Proud Scars

Proud Scars

Reflections of a Jewish Christian

DAVID HAROLD GODWIN

THE CHOIR PRESS

First published in the United Kingdom in 2016 by
The Choir Press

ISBN 978-1-910864-14-2

To Harold and Anne

Contents

Introduction:
Who Do I Think I Am?

I have unashamedly adapted the title of the BBC family history series *Who Do You Think You Are?* for my own ends, as it captures something about what I am about to say. Namely that in writing this mixture of memoir, biography and autobiography, I may find out a bit more about myself. Certainly, that has happened, to a degree, to the various celebrities in the TV series, so why not me? How much 'navel gazing' there will be remains to be seen, but examining one's upbringing and family history seems a valid way to embark on the task of examining oneself.

However, there are pitfalls of which I must be aware and which I must try to avoid. I am thinking about the tendency for an individual to avoid responsibility for his or her own actions and blame them on their upbringing or on their ancestors. It is very easy to put all the blame on the 'sins of the fathers'. That is not to say that in coming to

Lighting candles on the site of the Hellerburg camp, to commemorate those Jews who were forced to go there and subsequently to Auschwitz.

understand ourselves it is not profitable to understand our ancestors.

The reason for doing this is, quite simply, to put my family history down in writing. My son, William, suggested several years ago that I should do this, something I never did with my parents and now it is too late! Interest and curiosity about my forebears did not exist when I was a child and it is only now, as I get older, that I have become so inclined. Also, it has to be said that my parents, along with most people of their generation, were not keen to tell their story. However, with my mother at least, this was hardly surprising. It was a letter from the International Red Cross in November 1997 that galvanised me into more curiosity concerning my family history.

Pilgrimage to Dresden

*T*he letter I received in 1997 was trying to trace my mother, who by this time was bedbound in a nursing home in Wallingford, Oxfordshire. The International Tracing Service of the Red Cross had been unable to trace my mother but had managed to trace her son (my father had died in 1972). I will quote from the letter:

Re: Tracing request concerning Jewish individuals from Dresden or relations of individuals deported from Dresden to Concentration Camp Auschwitz on 2nd March 1943.

Dear Sirs,
Our office has received a tracing enquiry for the group of persons mentioned above. The inquirers are Mrs Ingrid Silverman and Mr Ulrich Teschner, both residing in Germany.

Mrs Silverman and Mr Teschner are planning a commemoration for the former persecutees of the National Socialist Regime in Dresden on 23rd November 1997 in cooperation with the Jewish Community Dresden and the City of Dresden.

Regarding this project, we have been informed that a 25 minutes long documentary film of 1942 has been found in Dresden which shows the deportation of Jews from the so-called 'Judenhauser' (houses for Jews) in Dresden to a labour camp nearby on 23rd November 1942. Investigations carried out there revealed that all persons shown in this film were arrested in Dresden on 27th February and deported to Auschwitz in the night of 2nd March 1943 where they arrived on the 3rd March 1943. 293 persons are said to have been deported with this transport and a few survived.

Therefore we are searching for survivors or their relatives, in order to inform them about the film which was found, to exchange information and to advise them on the forthcoming commemoration.

Hannah and myself talk to two other relatives who now live in Israel.

>Ms Stephanie MAGEN, born in Chemnitz on 2.2.1925, and her
>mother, Erna MAGEN nee HINZELMANN, born on 7.1.1898, also
>belong to this group of persons.
>In the course of our investigations, we have been able to ascertain that
>the sister respectively the daughter of the forenamed persons, Mrs
>Annelies Godwin . . .

My mother was unable to attend the proposed ceremony in
Dresden, but even if she had been well enough, she had no desire
to go and relive those last four months of her mother and her
sister's lives. How much she knew, I will never know. She did not
ask much about our visit. When she spoke to her cousin, Inge
Smith, who lives in Franklin, Tennessee in America, in a tape-
recorded message in March 1998, she said that our visit brought up

memories which she would rather not have. 'The whole business last year of bringing up times of over fifty years ago seems like a dream … it was quite a traumatic time for me and I was frightened for them to bring the past up, but I have digested it quite well.'

Remarkable understatement, yet a real fear that these ghastly events would also affect her children and grandchildren.

Ingrid Silverman was marvellous in making it possible for my daughter Hannah, William and myself to go to Dresden. She organised our accommodation in the Jugendgästehaus (youth hostel) in Dresden and also got the German railways to pay for our tickets from Berlin to Dresden and return. She got them to supply free tickets as it was the state railway that had transported our relatives to the concentration camps.

We flew to Tegel airport in Berlin, then made our way across the city to Lichtenberg station and then on to Neustadt station in Dresden. Ingrid was there to meet us and for the next two days took us in her car to the various meetings and events.

The morning after our arrival we met with the other 'pilgrims' at the site of the synagogue in Dresden. We were the only people from the UK. The others were from Israel, America and Germany; about two dozen of us. The purpose of our visit was to trace some of the places shown in the film and then to commemorate the 293 people who were rounded up fifty years ago and put into the Hellerberg camp before being transported to Auschwitz the following March.

The story of the discovery of the 8mm black-and-white film is quite interesting. It has only been since the destruction of the Berlin Wall in 1989, and so the fall of Communist East Berlin and the German Democratic Republic, that information and documents jealously guarded by the communist regime have been unearthed. So it was with this film.

On the 23rd November 1942 a photographer, Eric Hohne, was ordered to go to a 'Judenhaus' at No. 2 Sporergasse in Dresden and film the ordered evacuation of Jewish people from their homes and their transportation to a sort of holding camp, before being moved on to Auschwitz, going through a decontamination centre and then life in the Hellerberg camp. How Ingrid Silverman, a teacher from Berlin, and her husband, Ulrich Teschner, a film producer, discovered the film, I don't know, except that they came across the film in a shed belonging to Mr Hohne. They then began to identify some of the people captured in the film and so tell their stories.

The end results of Ingrid and Ulrich's extraordinary efforts were both a book and a video. The book is called *Auf den Spuren der Menschen der 'Judensiedlung' am Hellerberg in Dresden* (1997), recounting both the events of 23rd November 1942 to 3rd March 1943 and the background of the people involved. The video, *Die Juden sind weg* ('The Jews have gone'), tells the same story but also contains clips of the original film and interviews with eyewitnesses and survivors.

Two of these people are Henny Brenner and Henry Meyer, who both came on the pilgrimage to Dresden. Henry Meyer, who is a musician and lives in Cincinnati, Ohio, was one of the people who survived Auschwitz and remembered the Magen family. However Henny Brenner, who must have been the same age as Steffi Magen, remembered Steffi well as they both worked together in the Zeiss Ikon factory. This was forced labour where young people were conscripted to work on intricate electronic equipment as they were more dextrous. A quote from *Die Juden sind weg* (Ingrid and Ulrich had brought the original film to show to Henny Brenner to see who she recognised): 'That is Steffi Magen in the white smock, or whatever she is wearing, the daughter of the pharmacist Magen.'

We followed in Steffi and Erna's footsteps, and in those of Arthur Hinzelmann, Erna's brother who suffered the same fate. We visited the decontamination centre, which was now an almost derelict workshop: the aforementioned Zeiss Ikon works. This was empty but very much intact. A vast working area where machines and work benches once stood. The factory was very solidly built with special bombproof constructions to its outside walls, which countered the theory that Dresden was not of industrial and

We visited the former Zeiss Ickon works. Henny Brenner and Henry Meyer both knew the Magen family.

Listening to all the names being read out, William read the section containing his great gandmother and great aunt.

military value. We then all went to the site of the Hellerberg camp – nothing remains – and lit 273 candles, with different people reading out the names of those who had been ordered there. William read the list containing the names of his great-grand-mother and great-aunt. Finally we all assembled in the town hall for a reception and the premiere showing of *Die Juden sind weg*.

This short visit to Dresden brought home to my heart something that, up till then, I had only known about in my head. In other words, I knew something about my mother's incredible history but had somehow felt detached or emotionally uninvolved. Somehow this has changed, and partly because I experienced something about her family through third parties and independent sources. To hear other people talking about my family, to see a photograph of my mother with her sister and parents on holiday in nearby mountains in Czechoslovakia, the picture of Steffi in the film: all brought a new awareness to me.

Having the same effect, perhaps even more so, were the references to my mother's family in the diaries of Victor Klemperer. These remarkable diaries were an obvious source of information for Ingrid and Ulrich about the Jews living in Dresden during that time.

Victor Klemperer, 1881–1960 (who was the cousin of Otto Klemperer, the conductor), was a professor who managed to survive the Nazis and the Allied bombing. What is more, he secretly wrote these diaries which spanned the years 1933 to 1959, thus giving an important insight into the Germans and Germany at that time. Here is the entry for the 26th May 1942:

26th May, Tuesday morning

I did not leave the house over Whitsun. Only when it is absolutely necessary do I venture on to the street. – Towards midday Dr Glaser came for a short visit. In the afternoon, Steinitz. On Saturday he and his wife had innocently found themselves caught up in a house search while visiting acquaintances: punches to the back of the head.

I often heard of a Jewish pharmacist called Magen. The man was arrested several times. His 17-year-old son fled, as he was about to be evacuated, and evidently escaped. That was in January. As a result, the father, a 50-year-old, was arrested again, he was put in the familiar solitary confinement of the police cells. – Yesterday Kätchen tells us: 'Magen has died.' – 'One murder more!' – Kätchen almost indignant: 'But no! They don't do things like that at the Police Praesidium, they behave properly there. He simply had bad heart trouble and won't have got any care there.' So this is no longer considered a murder but a normal end.

I have written a short screenplay for a docu-drama based on the above. It is called *Father and Son* and I have included it as an appendix.

These diaries were only published in Berlin in 1995 and subsequently translated into English and abridged in 1999. As they were abridged I was curious to know whether there was any other information about my family which had not been published. I contacted the translator, Martin Chalmers, via Weidenfeld & Nicolson. Martin Chalmers put me in touch with the original German transcriber, Walter Nowojski. Mr Nowojski and I exchanged letters over several months in 2004. He had been a student of Victor Klemperer and had made it his life's work to transcribe the handwritten diaries for publication.

Eichwalde
5th January 2004

... I want to thank you most sincerely for your kind letter, which is of great interest to me. It has given me information about people which I otherwise only have been able to elicit by making painstaking enquiries.

For more than twenty years now I have been involved in the estate of Victor Klemperer. I began by transcribing his almost illegible hand-written East German diaries, having no plans then of actually publishing the material. Klemperer was my lecturer at university. So far I have deciphered all 16,000 hand written pages of the diaries ...

Martin Chalmers has abbreviated a lot of material for the English edition, some of which has to do with your family. Page 128 of the English edition of Weidenfeld and Nicolson 1999 begins with brackets. The paragraph which Chalmers omits, reads [dated 29th August 1942, Saturday forenoon], 'There was a Magen family. The head of which was a pharmacist. Father, son, mother and daughter worked at the Goehle-Works. The young lad, blond and strong, fled, as he should have gone to Riga in the January. The father was thrown into prison, the son captured and brought back to a concentration camp. The father died in prison after a few months. The young lad died in the concentration camp. Cause of death: stomach and intestinal catarrh. Since when does a fit young man die of that? Either typhoid or no doctor or by injection!' ...

I gained more information from the estate of Dr Willy Katz [he was the only doctor allowed to look after the Jews in Dresden at this time] and the latter revised and supplemented the deportation list dated 3rd March 1943. That was all to do with the interned Jews in the so called Hellerberg barracks.

The paragraph about the Magen family on this list goes:

Magen, Erna, born Hinzelmann, date of birth 7/1/1898 in Dresden; nationality German Reich; living 1939 Fürstenstasse 18, 1942: Altenzeller Strasse 26 (?); died in Auschwitz.
Magen, Stephanie, born 1/2/1925 in Chemnitz, nationality German Reich; died in Auschwitz.

A letter preserved in the Leo Baeck Institute in New York from Heinz (Henry) Meyer [the musician we met in Dresden] to Rudolf Apt, dated 9/9/1945, reads: 'Dr Magen was a pharmacist and has a large pharmacy in Chemnitz. The elder daughter lives in England. When the Riga transport should have left, only the son Claus, was on the list, since the rest of the family, father, mother and daughter Steffi, were working at Zeiss Ikon. Claus fled one night before the transport was due to leave and no-one found him for some time. Finally he was caught at the Swiss border and brought back to Dresden. On the same day Herr Magen was arrested. Claus was taken to Auschwitz after a short while and died there. Herr Magen suffered a heart attack and died of that. Frau Magen and Steffi were sent to Auschwitz with me and both perished in the camp.'
(Leo Baeck Institute, New York, Apt Collection, section 11, part 8)

All this 'third-party' information, although most of it not new, brought it home further to me what had actually happened to my mother's family. That the Nazis had murdered them and had stolen their considerable wealth.

When we returned to England, it was Hannah who raised the whole question: the total injustice that had happened and whether there was any way to seek compensation. My mother had received some compensation from the German government for the loss of her parents. This, I believe, happened in the early fifties and I suspect was only a nominal sum. What I do know is that Mum had a Dr Loeb, who was a lawyer in Stamford Hill. He managed her affairs and it was he who put her on to Frau Hanna Magen, the widow of the late mayor of Bonn, Karl Magen, who was a cousin of my mother's father. Mum told me that when she and I went to see Dr Loeb, some children called out (presumably to me) as we were entering his house, 'Little Yid'!

The story of how my sister and I received compensation is worth telling, if only because I achieved it on my own without the 'assistance' of a lawyer who no doubt would have charged a large fee. However, the whole process once again added to my knowledge about the Magen family and brought home to me even more how awful was the tragedy that befell them.

My first port of call was the Jewish Board of Deputies. I had had a little to do with this organisation when I had been a hospital chaplain. They supplied visitors for Jewish patients and indeed a Jewish chaplain. I will always remember my part-time colleague, Revd Schneider, the rabbi who used to come to the London Hospital, Whitechapel, from the Gants Hill synagogue.

Anyway, the Board of Deputies put me in touch with the Holocaust Educational Trust, which was in its infancy then. The Trust organises regular visits to Auschwitz especially for school-children. My main link with the Trust was Michael Newman, who was extremely helpful in the whole process. It was he who gave me essential information and advice on how to proceed, it was he who supported me in making some sort of claim from the German government, and it was he who put me on to the Conference of Jewish Material Claims against Germany, Inc. Needless to say there were many letters and phone calls between me and their office in Frankfurt.

There was a very long gap when I heard nothing. Then at the beginning of December 1998 I received the following letter:

Frankfurt am Main, December 7, 1998

Restitution/Compensation for Confiscated Property in Former East Germany
Goodwill Fund

Dear Mr Godwin
Referring to my last letter of September 28, 1998, I am happy to inform you that I just received the information from our Goodwill Fund section that based on your letter we have filed your application for three Goodwill Fund cases in our files. Your Goodwill Fund applications have been registered and for the further processing of these applications you are kindly asked to provide us with a certificate to prove your identity . . .

This was an incredible breakthrough as I had already been told that I was five years out of date in filing a claim! However there was this Goodwill Fund for those who had missed the boat. Then, in August 1999, I received another letter.

> *Frankfurt a. M., July 29, 1999*
>
> Property: **Kronenstrasse 1 in Chemnitz**
> **Schumannstrasse 8 in Chemnitz**
> **Infeld & Meyring in Dresden**
> Original owner: **Dr Kurt Magen**
>
> *Dear Mr Godwin,*
> *Firstly, I would like to confirm that we have registered the above property as so-called Goodwill cases. We have received the documents sent us . . .*
> *The facts of the matter in the restitution or compensation are as follows:*
> *Re Kronenstrasse 1 in Chemnitz our organisation was recognized as being eligible here. We received a compensation payment . . .*
> *Regarding the Schumannstrasse 8 in Chemnitz a decision was made . . .*
> *As far as I can tell from the document I have, the business asset consisting of the firm Infeld & Meyring, has not yet been dealt with by the property office responsible. However, in this case, we have nothing to show a connection with your grandfather, Dr Kurt Magen. Perhaps you could give us more details here. In principle payments can be made to you for the properties if you can prove that you are the heir of your grandfather, Dr Kurt Magen. Unfortunately the papers sent us are not sufficient. I have to ask you to apply for your grandfather's certificate of inheritance as well those of heirs who may have predeceased you . . .*

On first reading, there were feelings of both excitement and panic. Excitement that my mother's family was indeed very wealthy; panic that they were murdered, their property stolen, and hardly in a position to produce 'certificates of inheritance'. My mother had very little evidence of paperwork about her family. However she did have her original birth certificate, which did enable me to obtain a certificate of inheritance, through the German embassy in London, at a cost of £1,000. Michael Newman advised that I should contest this fee as it was for compensation money. I wrote to the German ambassador about this but got a letter from his office saying that was the rule and so he could not bend it.

The firm Infeld & Meyring was a silk importing business in Dresden, owned by my grandmother's parents, and as I write I have not been able to prove that my grandfather was the original owner even though the Claims Conference originally made this claim.

The Magen Family

My mother's father, Kurt Magen, was born on the 8th July 1882 in the town of Leobschütz, now Głubczyce, in Poland. Kurt was one of four children. His siblings were Ludwig, Elsa and Arthur. Ludwig and Arthur died in the First World War. Elsa and her husband settled in Belgium. Their father, Heinrich Magen, was the owner of a steam mill in the region, of which there were many. He later became mayor.

The industrial revolution was thriving in the area because of natural resources and accordingly successful industrialists flourished. Roman Catholicism was strong, but the church seemed to coexist fairly well with the synagogue.

The young Kurt Magen was sent to an evangelical elementary school in the nearby town of Ohlau. He then went to the Royal Catholic Gymnasium in Leobschütz. However, my mother told me that he argued with the priests (Jesuits) so his father moved him back to Ohlau, where he attended the City Gymnasium, and it was there that he obtained his higher education in humanities. He was a lieutenant in the First World War and was awarded the Iron Cross. In 1907 he passed the state examination in apothecary.

Kurt Magen studied at the University of Zurich and was awarded his doctorate on the 26th July 1912. His dissertation was entitled 'Contributions to the comparison of the

Kurt and Erna Magen.

My mother with her father Kurt, her mother Erna and her sister Steffi on a visit to Czechoslovakia.

anatomy of seed husks of a number of families of the Engler series of Sapindales', and it is the CV that accompanies this erudite work that has produced most of the aforementioned information. However I have more recently discovered via the Internet a record of his academic career from the records of the University of Zurich where he did his PhD. It seems that he first graduated at the University of Rostock and did an 'apprenticeship' at a chemist's in Schwerin.

It is interesting to have at this point, a brief look at the derivation of the name Magen. It is the German word for 'stomach', but perhaps more importantly it also comes from the Hebrew meaning 'shield' or 'star'. Thus the Magen David or Star of David. Also the Israeli equivalent of the Red Cross is Magen David Adom, which is Israel's national emergency, medical, disaster, ambulance and blood bank service. 'What's in a name?' we might ask. The name Magen does seem to have strong Jewish roots, but more about that later.

Kurt Magen worked for the pharmaceutical firm IG Faben: a cruel irony because it was they who supplied the gas for the extermination camps. He then built up his own pharmaceutical business in Chemnitz, which became very successful.

Kurt Magen was clearly a very clever scientist who achieved a comfortable lifestyle. His pharmaceutical works was at No. 1 Kronenstrasse in Chemnitz, where he developed various remedies, including a cream for getting rid of freckles. It must have been a sizeable place, judging from its value but also from a little story that I always remember from my mother. One of Dr Magen's employees came to tell him that there was a fire at the works. The only problem was that the man had a bad stammer and just could not get the words out. So my grandfather suggested that he should sing the message, which he duly did to a well-known German song. My mother sang the tune to me but I did not recognise it. But what quick thinking by her father.

Erna Magen (nee Hinzelmann)

Their house was also in Chemnitz, No. 8 Schumannstrasse, and by all accounts very comfortably furnished with good furniture and decoration and paintings. The family had a maid and the children, who were later sent away to school in St Gallen in Switzerland, had a nanny. My grandfather owned two cars: an Opel and a Fiat. Interestingly, virtually the only thing that my mother was able to have in England was her bicycle with a back-pedalling brake, made by Opel. I can remember riding this myself, when we lived in Great Yeldham in Essex. Otherwise everything that my mother's family owned was stolen by the Nazis.

In 1919, Kurt Magen married Erna Hinzelmann, the daughter of Eduard and Martha Hinzelmann. Eduard Hinzelmann ran a silk wholesale business in Dresden. It was called 'Gebrüder Hinzelmann' and later on was named 'Infeld & Meyring'. Erna Caroline was the youngest of four children (the others were Arthur, Trudie and Lucie) and was born on the 3rd December 1892.

I have a rather splendid photograph, which was given to me by

The Magen Family.

Lucie's daughter Igne, of a large family gathering in what looks like a sumptuous ballroom, presumably in Dresden. Martha is sitting in the front looking like the grande dame and two of her daughters, Erna and Lucie, are in a couple of rows behind, but there is no sign of Kurt. Maybe they had not married when the photo was taken.

By all accounts, Erna was a beautiful and elegant lady, who dressed well. Inge, her niece, described her as:

> … a very beautiful woman, who was always kind and much loved by her children. She often took her family to Dresden for visits with her parents and sisters and brother and also spent vacations with them in Czechoslovakia, the beach or in the Erz mountains for skiing.

When I think about it, this short account of my grandmother contains more information about my grandmother than I ever gleaned from my mother. I always got the impression that my mother Annelies was closer, at least in temperament, to her father rather than her mother. My mother was a rebel (she was nearly

Annelies

Steffi

expelled from boarding school for locking a teacher in a cupboard!) and seems to have been compared unfavourably with her pretty younger sister, Steffie. Inge, their cousin, played with Steffie as a child:

> … As Steffie and I were very close in age we used to play together a lot. Mostly we played ball on the steps leading from the veranda to the garden, but also played with the dolls which used to belong to our mothers and which were still there. The playroom had previously been a bedroom … Steffie had a particularly happy disposition. She could always see the funny side and we used to laugh a lot. She was a good student, too – intelligent and hardworking. Above all she was a very pretty girl and she was the darling of our grandmother [Martha Hinzelmann].

Steffie conformed and did all the right things whereas Annelies, who described herself as 'the ugly duckling' and 'a mongrel', went her own way – like her father. So, if there was some favouritism in the Magen household, it would not be totally surprising.

In fact, the way my mother received her name was not particularly auspicious. My grandfather was very keen to quickly register his daughter's birth, and when his wife asked him why he had chosen the name Annelies, he told her that he had once been engaged to a girl called Annelies!

My mother told me:

> We passed our childhood in a large comfortable house, wanting for
> nothing, cared for by nannies, seeing our parents at organised times
> … When my brother was born, my father told us that the stork had
> been to visit and brought us a little brother and that it had bitten my
> mother on the leg and that was why she was in bed. My father was
> part Jewish. He was a dark, square-set man, stubborn by nature; he
> would not change his mind or compromise his ideas once they were
> in place. He would not join Rotary or any of the local organisations
> for businessmen of which he strongly disapproved [although he did
> at some point get involved with the Masons, which would count
> against him when he was later arrested].

When my mother happened to burst into her father's study
and found him crying, she was deeply shocked. My mother's
cousin, Inge, described him as 'very stern' and she remembers
the scars he had on his face and of which he was very proud.
These scars not only showed that he had been to university but
also emphasised the German preoccupation with fencing and
duelling at the time.

In 1935, Kurt Magen went to South America in order to investi-
gate the possibility of exchanging his pharmacy with one over
there. However he decided that it was too small and so never
emigrated. How history would have been different! What this non-
episode does show is that he was a very proud man, who was not
going to easily let go of a large successful business which he had
built up even though, by that time, there was obvious threats both
to him and his family. He considered himself a loyal German who
contributed to German society. How far he was 'blind' to the
events going on around him is difficult to guess. Perhaps he
simply disregarded them and genuinely thought that he was not
going to be affected.

Annelies and Steffi attended the Girls' Academy in Marschner-
strasse in Dresden, but there came a point when they were not

allowed to attend there, so Dr Magen, ever resourceful, sent them to be educated in Switzerland. All three children were sent away to an international boarding school in St Gallen. Annelies was very sporty. She swam, took part in athletics and, of course, skied. A short-sighted girl managed to throw a javelin that hit my mother between the eyes.

My mother was told by her English teacher that she would never master the language. Little did she know that her prediction would be totally wrong. It was the Quakers in Somerset who helped my mother to learn English when she first came to England in 1938, and no doubt it was a matter of survival that drove my mother to conquer the language. She often had some curious expressions, which I picked up. She also spoke with a strong guttural accent (I think from Saxony), but I was never aware of it myself.

Annelies had a close school friend who was like-minded. Her name was Marianne Simon and she came from South Africa. I can remember receiving food parcels from Marianne just after the war when many items were still rationed, not least chocolate! I can also remember Marianne visiting us in Great Yeldham, Essex, and obligingly mending my plastic rifle, grumbling, I seem to remember, that my mother should be doing this. She then moved to Zimbabwe, where she married a British engineer who helped to build the Kariba Dam. When she died my mother inherited some money and jewellery from Marianne, although I think the Zimbabwean government took a fair whack.

In about 1937/8 my grandfather was forced to bring his children back to Germany when he was forbidden to send any more money out of the country in order to pay for their education.

Events from now onwards took a rapid downward turn for the Magen family and one can only imagine what horror they went through. As I have already mentioned, my mother has never spoken comprehensively about what happened, not that she necessarily knew everything anyway as she was sent to England in 1938. What is evident is that under the growing chaotic circumstances, knowledge of the facts is inevitably confused and there is inevitable speculation.

When my mother and her brother and sister returned to Germany from Switzerland, the authorities accused my mother of being a spy and threatened her with a 'labour camp' if she did not leave the country. This was obvious further pressure on her parents, but Dr Magen, characteristically, refused to cooperate with the authorities; anyway, where could Annelies go? However, Erna, her mother, in desperation spoke to the British consul's wife, with whom she played bridge in Dresden. An entry visa to the UK was obtained as long as she did 'useful' work such as nursing. So it was that an 18-year-old girl with hardly any English flew from Berlin airport to Croydon with just a small suitcase. Her trunk and bicycle followed later to Victoria station. This was obviously a private arrangement as Annelies was too old to go on the Kindertransport.

In the meantime the family had moved from Chemnitz to Dresden: 18 Fürstenstrasse, previously owned by Martha Hinzelmann (Erna's mother), who died on the 10th April 1937. I have this information from the 'announcements section' of the Dresden equivalent to the *Jewish Chronicle,* but some of the details which follow of the Magen family story are open to hypothesis and speculation.

What is quite likely is that the Magen family were forced to move from their house at Schumannstrasse in Chemnitz as Dr Magen's business was taken by the Nazis and given to their own people. I cannot imagine that Kurt Magen moved to Dresden voluntarily, as he had a perfectly good house in Chemnitz! However, it does seem that Kurt Magen acquired the deeds of this house as far back as 1930. Whether he was the 'original owner' of the silk importing business as claimed by the Claims Conference is subject to speculation.

Latterly (c. 1937), Infeld & Meyring (previously called 'Gebrüder Hinzelmann') employed twelve people, comprising two managers, one secretary, seven salesmen and two travelling salesmen, with a turnover of 500,000.00 RM.

I would like to quote at length a letter written on 31st July 2000 by Dr Ute-M. Babick-Kruger on behalf of the Claims Conference:

> ... Now for your questions. After having had a look at the evidence from the Companies Register, a copy of which I enclose, I have to tell you that I can unfortunately not confirm that Dr Kurt Magen was the owner of the firm Infeld and Meyring. Two others are listed as owners: Max Infeld and Walter Meyring. The company was situated at 2 Wettinerstr., was liquidated in 1934 and the firm was deleted from the Companies Register. Both the original owners were after 1934 employed as company representatives, with Max Infeld at 7 Broad Street and Walter Meyring at 22 Brother Lane.
>
> The deeds of 18 Fürstenstr. were as you know, acquired by Dr Kurt Magen in 1930 from Martha Hinzelmann, nee Kohn, the widow of David Hinzelmann. In the deeds was a mortgage for the banking house Philipp Elimayer for upward of 40,000 RM, which possibly resulted from the (obligation) indebtedness of the undermentioned Hinzelmann brothers. This is, however, speculation. After Dr Kurt Magen acquired the deeds, the mortgage was quashed in 1931.
>
> As you have rightly established, the owners of the firm Hinzelmann Brothers were Arthur Hinzelmann and Wilhelm Perlberg. We could not find a company share owned by Dr Kurt Magen hitherto. Although we have no company registration document to hand, there are other pieces of evidence to the effect that the undertaking had been liquidated at any rate before 1937. I am somewhat puzzled, too, that it had been sold, since in 1937 it was at 21 King John Street, whereas Hinzelmann Brothers at 1, Obergeschoss was for rent as a residence, with no further comparable use. The new tenants were, according to the address book of 1937, a doctor and members of the NSDAP.
>
> As soon as I have to hand the full Companies Register details on the Hinzelmann Brothers company, I shall write to you again with more precise details of the firm's dissolution.
>
> Until then I remain yours in the hope that each one of your questions can be addressed as fully as possible.
>
> Yours sincerely,
> Dr Ute-M. Babick-Kruger

I did not receive any further information from Dr Babick-Kruger. When I wrote in 2000 to Inge, my mother's cousin in Franklin, Tennessee, to see if I could get any more information about the silk business, she was very adamant that my grandfather had no claim on it.

21st May 2000

> *... Now to Infeld and Meyring. It was a silk-wholesale business, but it belonged strictly to my father and his partner and the German government paid him reparations years ago. My grandfather's business was named 'Gebrüder Hinzelmann', if I remember correctly. Arthur Hinzelmann and Willy Perlberg ran the business after my grandmother's death in October 1937, or even before that. My grandfather died in 1922. I wish you the best of luck as you claim compensation, but not from the business Infeld and Meyring. I know that my grandmother gave Kurt Magen her house on Fürstenstrasse, but when I visited Dresden in 1985 I did not find it. It must have been destroyed in the bombing ...*

Walter Meyring, Inge's father, was the son of Michaelis Cohn, who came from Gorlitz. When he came to Dresden he changed his name to Meyring, presumably to detract from his Jewish roots. Walter married Lucie, the daughter of David and Martha Hinzelmann, which gave him an introduction into the silk importing business.

Arthur Hinzelmann was born on the 3rd July 1888 in Dresden and died in 1943 in Auschwitz. He also was rounded up by the Nazis in 1942 and sent to the Helleberg camp from the 'Judenhaus' at 6 Cranachstrasse in Dresden.

Arthur was the eldest of four children. His sisters were Erna Magen, Trudie Perlberg and Lucie Meyring. He never married and lived with his mother (Martha) at 18 Fürstenstrasse. It seems he was a jovial person and there is a picture of him, taken in 1921, looking very dapper along with his sister and brother-in-law (Lucie and Walter Meyring – Inge's parents). Inge says of Arthur, 'His presence always brought life into the house; he enjoyed life, was interested in horse racing and liked a glass of beer.' When the Magen family moved into Fürstenstrasse he moved to the house in Cranachstrasse. From what my mother has said he was not a good businessman and it is possible that as a result my grandfather may have stepped in to save the business. However, as has already been indicated, this is hypothetical.

We need now to try and trace the harrowing events that beset the Magen family from 1938 to 1943. This is going to be difficult as my mother, who was already in England at this time and having to survive as an alien in a foreign country alone without her family, did not speak much about what happened to her parents, brother and sister. Not that she necessarily knew much anyway. I do not know how much correspondence there was between her and her family at this time. Possibly not much. There was a war between the two countries, after all, and her family were being forced to live under increasing restrictions. It seems that any letters that my mother did receive, she destroyed at a later date.

A still from the 8mm film showing Steffi who assisted Dr. Katz in the Hellerburg camp.

A 'mug-shot' of Claus in Auschwitz.

As far as I know it was the Red Cross who communicated the awful news of the death of her family, but not, it seems, concerning her mother and sister.

In December 1945, my mother contacted the Search Bureau of World Jewish Relief. I have a copy of the registration slip (but no file) made out in 1949. My mother wrote from Stepney Rectory just five months after I was born, in order to locate her mother and sister 'missing in the Holocaust'. There is no other information.

Claus Magen.

This somewhat sparse information is, however, very important, as it indicates that as late as 1945 my mother had had no information about the fate of her mother and sister. She had just given birth to her first child, yet she was unable to share this news with the women of her family. The pain she must have gone through is inconceivable. In desperation she must have contacted the Jewish organisation, but to no avail.

As I write this (November 2010) there is no written evidence that my grandmother and aunt went to

Auschwitz and I wonder whether my mother ever was formally told about their fate.

A letter from the Jewish Relief Archive, written on the 1st November 2010, simply says:

> *... It would appear that ... Anneliese Magen was brought to Britain by an organization other than ours (probably by the Society of Friends, the Quakers) whose war-time files no longer exist today ...*

In 1941, Kurt, Erna, Steffi and Claus were forced to go and live in a 'Judenhaus' at 26 Altenzellerstrasse. From there Erna and Steffi were moved to the barrack camp in the Hellerberg and forced to work at the Zeiss Ikon works. I have already referred to the fate of my grandmother and aunt in Auschwitz. Apparently there was an eyewitness account of them both avoiding the gas chambers but throwing themselves on the electrified wire.

On the 6th September 2010, I visited Auschwitz and was able to obtain the 'death certificate' of Claus from the archives there. Claus died on the 16th August 1942. The cause of his death was recorded as acute gastroenteritis. This may well not be true as it was a convenient diagnosis which was automatically recorded for most people. Certainly the relatively small size of the camp and the thousands of people crammed together would have lent itself to rife infection and disease. However, Claus was a fit young man able to work. My speculation, on his past record, is that he was disobedient or tried to escape and was executed in some unspeakable way.

I was very interested to see that Claus was registered as 'evangelisch', formerly 'mosaisch', which indicates that the Magen family were baptised and accounts for the Lutheran hymn book which belonged to my mother and which I have in my possession now. However, this did not stop Hitler pursuing his madness. All German Jews were forced to have a Hebrew name. Thus, Kurt Israel Magen, Erna Sara Magen and Claus Joachim Eduard Israel Magen.

There were no records of either Erna or Steffi in the Auschwitz archives. Looking at the substantial electric fence surrounding the camp makes me think that they did not wait to be murdered and committed suicide soon after they arrived there on the 3rd March 1943, and so did not give the authorities time to 'register' them in any way. However, there is anecdotal evidence (from Tante Hanna, I think) that while they were there, and I would presume in Block 11, which was the women's section, Erna was seen looking after her fellow prisoners.

Now that I have a clearer idea of the order of events concerning Kurt, Erna, Steffi and Claus, I can speculate on what happened. They all were ordered to live in a 'Judenhaus', which was Altenzellerstrasse No. 26, in Dresden. Kurt was arrested several times and spent time in the police prison in Dresden. In the meantime Claus escaped from transport to Riga, was arrested and was ultimately sent to Auschwitz, where he met his death on 16th August 1942. Kurt, while in prison, met his death sometime just before 26th May 1942. On the 23rd November 1942, Erna and Steffi were rounded up and incarcerated in the Hellerberg camp, where Steffi had to work in the Zeiss Ikon works.

Inge Smith takes up the story. I quote from her auto-biography *Born for America*:

Annelies Magen as a teenager in better times.

Steffani, a beautiful girl, still in her youth, and closer to my age, was taken to the Zeiss factory in Hellerberg along with my Aunt Erne and her brother, my Uncle Arthur. There, Steffani worked alongside a Jewish physician by the name of Dr Katz.

The fact that he was married to a non-Jewish woman allowed him the opportunity to remain at the factory camp in Hellerberg even after many others were sent to Auschwitz. Katz was given the responsibility of examining every labor prisoner brought to the Zeiss factory. My cousin Steffani became his assistant and remained with him until she was ultimately sent to Auschwitz with her mother and uncle.

They were transported on the 2nd/3rd March 1943 to Auschwitz, where they met their deaths soon afterwards.

I have already written the docu-drama *Father and Son*, which is about the fate of Dr Magen and his son Claus, but it is inevitably a combination of fact and fiction. I will now try and give the facts as much as possible, with the help of the eyewitness account of Henry Meyer, who not only was rounded up on the 23rd November 1942 but also survived Auschwitz.

9th September 1945

> *Herr Magen was a pharmacist and had a big chemist shop in Chemnitz. I'm reporting this because the eldest daughter lives in England. When the transport to Riga was about to set off, only the son, Claus, was on the list of people to be deported because the rest of the family, father, mother and daughter, Steffi[,] were working for Zeiss-Ikon. Claus escaped on the night before the transport set off and was not found for a while. Finally he was caught at the Swiss border and brought to Dresden. On the day Claus was caught, Herr Magen was arrested. Nobody knew the reason. Shortly afterwards, Claus was taken to Auschwitz, where he perished. Herr Magen suffered a fatal heart attack in jail. Frau M. and Steffi were taken to Auschwitz, as I was, and both perished there.*

It was Henry Meyer who wrote this on the 9th September 1945, although I cannot work out to whom he is writing. I wonder whether there is a misprint and the date should be 9th September *1995*, when Henry Meyer would have written to Ingrid Silverman from his home in the USA in reply to her research. It is inevitable that there should be confusion about these events, not only because war is confusing but also because the memory is confused, not surprisingly, when one tries to come to terms with the whole ghastliness of the situation.

Kurt Magen was sent to Buchenwald concentration camp as early as 1938. The records say that he went there on 11th November 1938 and was released on the 1st December 1938. His prisoner number was 23282 and his category 'Aktions-Jude'. We also have a copy of his 'Fund Managing Card' – a sort of time sheet.

His son Claus, who was apprenticed to a locksmith, was deported to Riga but escaped possibly more than once. I have details from the International Tracing Service of the Red Cross, which state that Claus Magen was in custody on the 7th April 1942 in the Leipzig police prison – his number 5486. On one occasion, he managed to get to Tante Hanna's (Hanna Magen's) house and then escape to Switzerland. However, he was told that if he didn't give himself up and return to Dresden, the authorities would kill his father. This Claus did, only to be transported to Auschwitz and to discover that his father had died in prison.

I have been able to obtain the crematorium records from the archives in Dresden which state that Kurt Magen (No. 86257) died on the 23rd May 1942, that his body was cremated on 1st June 1942 and that his ashes were interred on the 3rd June 1942 in the 'Israelitischen Friedhof' in Dresden. The records also state that he died by 'Erhängen' (hanging). It looks like he committed suicide.

England

I now will try to give an account of my mother's time in England once she arrived in 1938 as an 18-year-old girl with very little English. Once again my knowledge is sketchy as she did not talk much about what must have been a horrendous time for her, to say the least. I think the idea was that her parents and siblings would follow her to England and get on a boat at Liverpool and go to Australia, but this wasn't to be. All I do know is that she was allowed to come here on condition that she did some work that would benefit the country, which was to be nursing, and that she was registered as an alien.

There was a cousin of her father's who was already living in London. Her name was Eleanor Ausberg. I can remember visiting her in an apartment in Lambeth quite near the Imperial War Museum when I must have been about five or six. Aunt Eleanor was an imposing lady who lived in some style. Her late husband was a lawyer who was well connected in German high society (pre-Hitler). She had a daughter, Renate, who moved to New York and married another lawyer by the name of Hunter and as far as I know is still there.

It seems that Annelies did not stay with Aunt Eleanor, although she was put up in a five-star hotel for a short while. What did happen is that she went to live with some Quakers in Somerset who taught her English. I have not been able to find any records of this time of my mother's life from the Society of Friends, maybe because this was a private arrangement. Certainly the Quakers did help, rather than the Jewish community either here or in America. There is speculation that if the Magen family had been able to get some sort of affidavit from relatives who had already been able to get to America, this account would be different. Again it is conjectured that as Dr Magen was a strong character, he may not have endeared himself to some of his relatives for whatever reason, and when the chips were down they were not prepared to help him.

However there was one person, Frau Hanna Magen, who I am sure would have helped Dr Magen if she and her husband, Karl, had been able. But they had their own problems, not only with Hitler but also with the Russians who were advancing into their home in Silesia. So I will digress for a moment and return to Germany.

Tante Hanna (as we always called her) was a remarkable lady, one of the first female lawyers in Germany. She and her husband and their son Albrecht lived in Silesia and she was able latterly to give my mother further information about our family. Again I have very little information, but I gather that Tante Hanna's family hid British airmen who were shot down. Also Claus on one of his 'escapes' turned up at their house and the young Albrecht had to be restrained from telling his friends about his 'adventurous' older cousin.

As has already been mentioned, Karl became mayor of Bonn, but I never met him. However we did meet Tante Hanna and Albrecht several times, both in Germany and in England. Here is a rather stilted translation of 'Portrait of the day', which appeared in a Bonn newspaper on her 80th birthday, 29th January 1981.

> Since the end of the War, Hanna Magen was very busy helping refugees, especially women, who had been driven from their homeland. She celebrates her 80th birthday today in Bonn. This woman came from Silesia and lived in Oppein and Breslau. She made herself a name, and through activity on international boards for eviction and refugee organisations, her influence outreached the borders of Bonn. Hannah Magen studied Law, History and the History of Art. She worked as junior barrister in a court of justice. She gave up her work when she married Karl Magen, the alderman of a county court, who later became mayor of Bonn. She was exposed to social problems in her youth. She accompanied her

My mother and father on their wedding day at St. Dunstan's Church, Stepney.

mother to her activities in day-nurseries for working mothers and this engagement with women stayed with her. Hannah Magen led in many social establishments, e.g. the National Society for Women, the Red Cross and in sewing workshops for soldiers and military hospitals in the First World War and in childcare.

Through her parents and her own activities, Hanna Magen became politically involved. This showed especially in the first years of the War when it was necessary to find work for the expelled. Dr Lukaschek, who founded the Society for the Expelled in West Germany, went to Hanna Magen to found a similar organisation for women. The aim was to help those expelled women who were hit hardest and worked especially hard. This was done in cooperation with new German societies for women. After the first beginnings, Hanna Magen changed from working on the coalface to being on the boards for the expelled in the ministries for the building of accommodation for those who had been expelled. Later she was delegated to international boards.

She was awarded the Order of Merit for assisting people who had come from East Germany. At her birthday reception, which was held at the old people's home called the Augustinum, the flow of guests did not stop. This is because Hanna Magen not only looked for contacts with people but is a woman whom society has to thank.

Albrecht, her son, also studied law and became a prominent politician in the city of Frankfurt, specialising in 'multicultural affairs'. He died in 2006. I quote from his obituary in the *Frankfurter Allgemeine*:

Magen was born ... the son of a Jewish father and a Catholic mother in 1929 in Wroclaw. After the expulsion, he began to study law in Jena, but went to West Germany in 1948. In Frankfurt, he completed his studies and received a doctorate ... When he was honoured two years ago with the Great Order of Merit, he said that 'The attention of strangers is an essential part of mainstream culture in Germany – as a consequence of the Biblical principle of "love thy neighbour as thyself".'

I will return to Anneliese Magen in England from 1938. Once she had acquired some English, she went up to the Chester Royal Infirmary to work as a nurse. However, during the evacuation at Dunkirk in 1940, all aliens had to leave sensitive places. As Chester was a garrison town, my mother had to leave and found herself working in a seedy nursing home in Wrexham, north Wales.

During the London Blitz, the cry went out for as many nursing staff as possible to come to London and help. So it was that she ended up in Mile End Hospital, an LCC hospital in the East End. It must have been around this time that she heard about the death of her family and one does not need to stretch one's imagination as to what it must have been like for her. The intense grief and isolation that she endured is unimaginable. Yet she survived.

She made friends with her nursing colleagues, notably Anne Hill and various boyfriends. Two that I know about are a police inspector who was married and a Jewish young man who was in some way connected with Marks & Spencer. It seems that they were quite serious but when he took Annelies to meet his parents, they put a stop to their relationship. The reason being that she was 'not Jewish enough'! This could not have helped the confidence of this young German refugee trying to make her way in war-torn London. As an alien she had to report regularly to Bow Street police station and evidently she had no support from the Jewish community.

My mother was unable to complete her nursing training at Mile End Hospital, as on the 27th April 1943 she married the hospital chaplain, Harold Frank Godwin. In those days nurses in training were not allowed to be married, so she opted to give up her job and they were married at

Mum with me circa. 1945.

St Dunstan's Parish Church, Stepney, with her friend Ann in attendance. The medical superintendent of the hospital, Dr Gordon Sears, gave her away. So she started a new life married to an Anglican priest living in a flat in St Dunstan's Rectory, Whitehorse Lane, Stepney, with German bombs falling all around her. On 8th August 1945, she gave birth to a son – the writer – in Mile End Hospital.

I was sent by Bob Hill (Ann Hill's husband) a letter written by my father during the war years to Ann, and I would like to quote it in full as it gives not only an insight into my father but also a snapshot of those war years in London and how life had to go on.

Stepney Rectory
E1
19.9.44

My Dear Ann,
Poor old girl, I am so sorry you have been feeling badly, and I hope you are better now.

So glad you have done so well with your exams. Pamela Hook's banns were called for the second time this morning.

Now about these photos. I have given the order as desired and asked that they should be sent to you. I took the liberty of telling them to send the bill to me. Now don't be furious. I am sure you are clenching your fists and longing to use them on me. But thank goodness I am beyond your range. Anyhow will you regard the photos as our Wedding present. Thank you. Row over.

Anne says can she see you this week either come to you or meet in town. Phone if you like STE 4120, not Monday evening.

Keith paid us a visit yesterday. He had us in fits, taking off one of the Doctors at the German Hospital.

The parson I referred Bob to is Rev. Hood. Vicar of Locking Parish Church.

I celebrated the Holy Communion at Mile End today. First Service there since the bomb fell.

We had a grand time at Cornwall. Swam every day. Feel much better now. I had to come back early to take the funeral of a friend of mine. We hope to go to Bristol for a week soon.

Love from us both to both of you
Harold and Anne.

The Godwin Family

My father, Harold Frank Godwin, was born on the 8th July 1915 in Bath, Somerset, the eldest son of Frank William and Ethel Godwin. They subsequently had my uncle Dennis (whom we knew as Dendo) and aunt Edith. Their father Frank was by all accounts a hard-working man who owned a hardware shop in Coombe Down in Bath. It was (and as far as I know still is) on a bend in the road and was known as 'Godwin's Corner'. My grandfather put his hand to various other occupations, namely removals, upholstery and even undertaking. In fact his occupation as recorded on my parents' wedding certificate is 'Upholsterer'.

I never knew my grandfather, who died before I was born from, it has been said, 'overwork'. He was the son of Albert Godwin and Hester Maggs, who had eight children: Frank, Wilfred, Jessie, Jack,

My grandmother, Ethel Godwin with my father Harold and his sister Edith.

My grandfather, Frank Godwin with my dad.

Ida, Sidney, Arthur and Reginald, who was considerably younger. Jack, Arthur, Ida and Sidney emigrated to Canada in 1908 and died there. Whether Wilfred went out there for a time, I don't know, but he married Rose Wells in London (I can just remember 'Auntie Rose'), and their daughter Olive lived latterly in Congleton, Cheshire. Jessie married Albert Bethel in Bath and I also remember them both. The other daughter, Ida, who went to Canada, married and moved to the north of the country and died in mysterious circumstances (murdered?).

My grandfather Frank, who also went out to Canada, joined the Canadian army and served under General Allenby in Palestine. He would have stayed in Canada as well, but Ethel (my grandmother) did not want to go, so he came back to Bath, where he built up his business: Godwins Ltd. They lived in Longfellow Avenue, Bath.

Ken Godwin (the son of Reg), who lives in Victoria, BC, wrote to me in 2005:

> I do know something of your G.D. from things my Dad told me. Frank was his favourite brother. He told me many times that your Dad, Harold, was a prince of a fellow. He thought the world of him.

Part of the Godwin business in Bath.

When we were over there in 1937 Frank hoisted me onto his shoulders and carried me around. After WWI my Dad worked for Frank at his hardware store and other activities. My dad talked of hauling carpets up to Beacham Cliff and beating them as a service to Frank's customers. My Dad was not too robust at that time after 4 years in the desert and coming down with malaria. He didn't see any future in it and decided to come to Canada where 2 of his brothers were (Sid and Jack).

Frank was a faithful member of St Luke's Church in Bath. The report of his funeral was entitled 'Mr F.W. Godwin – Loss to a Bath Parish' and amongst the floral tributes were 'Vicar of St Luke's Church and the Parochial Church Council: St Luke's Youth Church Council: Children and Teachers of St Luke's Sunday School'.

Frank was cremated at Arno's Vale, Bristol, and his ashes were scattered in the Garden of Rest at Arno's Vale.

His parents were Albert Godwin (1853–1929) and Hester Maggs (1853–1934). They married in Bath on the 27th September 1879 and lived in Norfolk Terrace in Bath. Albert worked as a chair maker and upholsterer. His father was George Godwin, born in 1821, and George's wife was, I think, Elizabeth, who was born in 1827. Although I have not proved this conclusively, I think that George Godwin's parents were John Godwin, born in Bath in 1791, and Sopha, born also in Bath in 1776.

My grandmother, Ethel, was born in December 1879 in Bristol and died of throat cancer in a London hospital in January 1939. She was the daughter of William Frederick Curtis, who was born in 1854 in Chewton Mendip, Somerset, and worked as a baker in Bristol. He married an Emily Jane Denman (1857–1889) from Bath.

I never knew any of my grandparents and cannot remember my father speaking of his parents much, and I regret not asking him more questions about his family. There is, however, one distant relative whom we knew as Uncle Alec. I never met him; at least I do not remember meeting him, and I think he was related to Hester Maggs, who married Albert Godwin. How he knew my parents I really don't know, but he must have known them well

Dad at Clifton Theological College, Bristol (back row, 2nd from right).

enough as he remembered me and my sister in his will. I quote from his last will and testament, dated 3rd September 1957:

Alexander William Charles Bennett of Green Gables Shrivenham in the County of Berks . . .

(b) To retain and invest the sum of Seven thousand pounds and to pay or apply the income thereof for the education, training and advancement of such of the two children of Harold Frank Godwin, the Rector of Great Yeldham David and Barbara as shall survive me with power to my Trustees to use the capital as well as the income thereof if in their absolute discretion they shall think fit and subject thereto for such of the said children as shall attain twenty one years of age and if there are two of them equally between them.

Harold Frank Godwin

Uncle Alec was a doctor and he was the medical officer for the GWR. He never married and he invested his money wisely. Why he was so generous to my parents and to us is a mystery. He also left a lovely Victorian silver tea set to my mother which is now with Hannah. Uncle Alec died on the 15th April 1972.

Returning to my father, Harold: he, along with Edith and Dendo, was brought up in a God-fearing household in Bath. Harold went to King Edward's School, Bath, and also helped his father in the business. I think he became a lay reader and worked for a time in Radstock, a coal-mining town in Somerset. He obviously had a vocation to the priesthood and went to Clifton Theological College (now Trinity) near the zoo in Bristol. He was ordained in St Paul's Cathedral in 1938 and went to serve his first curacy at All Hallows, Bromley-by-Bow in London. From there he went to serve his second curacy under Fr. Reginald French at St Dunstan's Church, Stepney. It was while saying Evensong in St Dunstan's that a bomb fell on the church, smashing a window and causing my father to leap over the pews to escape injury.

He was a member of the Home Guard and one of his duties was to guard an unexploded bomb until it was made safe. My mother told me that that they wanted to award him the George Cross, but he refused it. There was an independent, unconventional streak in my father. Going to serve in the East End must have been quite a contrast from Somerset, and then his marriage to a German Jewish refugee during the war must, I imagine, have been quite a shock to his family.

My parents could not have been more different, but they loved and complemented each other. Perhaps my father saw in my mother someone who was 'exotic' and she saw in him a security that she must have been crying out for. It was war time; neither of them knew whether they would survive. If they had lived in other circumstances … well, they would not have met and married. However, they did fall in love and got married and their marriage lasted until 1972 (29 years), when my father died.

Harold, Edith and Dendo.

Uncle Dendo during the war. He was forced marched as a POW from Italy to Poland.

Harold and Anne

My parents moved in about 1946 to Rayners Lane in Ruislip, North London, where my father had a position of priest in charge to a mission church, St Andrews. It is sometime at this point that I have my earliest recollections – playing with a large toy London bus.

In 1948 my sister Barbara Ruth was born and soon afterwards the whole family moved to Beckton, near East Ham. Again I think my father was a priest in charge, this time of the 'conventional district of St Michael'. St Michael's Church had been bombed and my father's church was again a mission church in a converted hall.

We lived in a purpose-built brick rectory very close to Beckton Gas Works. I do remember playing on the huge slag heaps nearby (much to my mother's distress) and also going with my father to collect coke from the gas works in a converted pram. It was here that I went to my first school – Windsor School, down towards the Royal Docks. I also remember ration books, receiving food parcels from South Africa, and the death of King George VI.

By the time of the coronation of Elizabeth II, we had moved to Great Yeldham in north Essex, where my father was rector until 1962. From there he moved to become rector of Orsett, also in the Chelmsford diocese. He was also chaplain to Orsett Hospital, a post which he enjoyed, and it was in 'his' hospital that he died on 5th November 1972. However, he was able to see me ordained priest in Southwark Cathedral on 1st October 1972 and, subsequently, my first Communion at St Philip with St Mark's, Camberwell, where I was a curate. The following is an extract of a letter that he wrote to me following that service.

The Rectory,
Orsett,
Grays, Essex
RM16 3JT
7th October 1972

My dear David,
This has been a great week and we have loved it . . .
   Yes, Thursday was great. You know your stuff and do it well.
   Bless you. Continue in the way you have started. It is marvellous to hear your people refer to 'our David'. The choice of hymns was fine. 'Come Holy Ghost' – of course. I associate 'Forth in Thy Name' with you. Mum loved Luther's strong tune. Your grandparents approve of 'Just as I am' and we all can sing 'Alleluia sing to Jesus' again and again . . .

The rector's wife was, of course, my mother. As children she was 'our mother'. A truism, maybe, but from a child's perspective I did not appreciate what it must have been like for her to settle and conform to such an establishment as the Church of England! Her story so far is worthy of a book or a film, but her role as a rector's wife is, on reflection, just as amazing. Knowing as much as I do now about my mother's past, it is extraordinary to contemplate what it was like for this German Jewish refugee, who came from a very privileged background, without any of her family and with very little money (a curate's pay was meagre). However, she did have the love and security of my father, a house to live in and two children to bring up. We were her priority and the affairs of the parish took second place.

That is not to say that she did not get involved in the parish. She was the enrolling member (chairperson) of the Mothers' Union; she was a member of the Women's Institute (I can remember her now, acting in a play in the Reading Room of Gt Yeldham); she organised fêtes and jumble sales at the rectory. These are just a few examples.

My parents (fifth and sixth from the left) on leaving Gt. Yeldham, Essex.

Later on, when we had moved to Orsett, she took up nursing again and became a state-enrolled nurse. She worked in Tilbury and Orsett Hospitals. Although I personally have no evidence of my mother suffering racial prejudice from the parishioners, it must have been strange both for her and for them. My mother had a very strong German accent. What I do know is that some people murmured about my mother going to be a nurse. This was not the sort of occupation for the rector's wife.

How my mother must have laughed to herself. Little did they know what she had left behind. And, indeed, that is what my mother had to do. To leave her old life behind and embrace her new life, not just in order to survive but also to make the most of what she did have. To look forward rather than backward. But how much she suppressed, one can only speculate.

Although she was generally very fit – she always liked swimming and was very good at it – she did latterly succumb to rheumatoid arthritis, and it is possible that this horrible disease was triggered off by my father's untimely death. When he died, my mother had three months to get out of Orsett Rectory and so in a very real sense became a refugee again. She had to get rid of most of her possessions once again in order to downsize and find a living-in job. She found a fairly unsatisfactory post in some sort of care home, run by the Red Cross in Brockley, South London. However she was able to find another post as assistant matron in Moulsford, now in Oxfordshire, which she enjoyed. During this time she bought a delightful (but not very practical) cottage in nearby Wallingford. The organisation for which she worked had the splendid title of 'The Friends of the Elderly and Gentlefolks Association'!

My mother Annelies Godwin.

When she was unable to manage the stairs in her cottage, she moved to some sheltered housing in the town. She ended her days in a very plush nursing home, Rush Court, also in Wallingford, and she died on the 19th December 1998. A BBC TV crew interviewed and filmed her while she was at Rush Court, but I have not heard whether the interview was ever broadcast. Her funeral was held at St Leonard's Church, Wallingford, on the 30th December 1998, and I quote here in full the tribute by the priest in charge at the time:

Funeral: Annelies Godwin
30/12/98

We celebrate today a life well lived; a life lived in support of home and family; but a life lived through and despite many difficulties. Annelies was born in Germany at just the wrong time in history. Just at the point when she might reasonably have expected to enjoy all the normal things of society for a woman in her late teens, the dark clouds of Nazi persecution of Jews forced her to flee to England.

It cannot have been easy to be uprooted from family and friends, from all that life promised; to find yourself in a country where you needed to learn another language and to begin a new life almost alone; it was a tough experience and one that in later life she preferred not to talk about too much. But Annelies was a courageous person and she was very much her own person; she had humour and she was positive and strong and I guess that much of that strength came from her early difficult experiences of settling in England and making a new life for herself.

She began nursing training and moved to continue her training at the Mile End Hospital in the East End of London. Happily there was a young chaplain named Harold who was to become her life long husband; it cannot have been easy for anyone to become the wife of a vicar in the East End in the post war period – let alone one who came out of Germany and who was cut off from her own closest family. That she was able to do this successfully, to support Harold in his work as if she had been a native and to rear their own young family is surely a tribute to her strength and positive approach to life. It was her nursing that brought her to work at the Old Vicarage at Moulsford in the years after Harold's death and then to settle in Wallingford.

I only had the privilege of meeting Annelies in the last two years of her life – and I do count it as a privilege to have known her. When the going was tough for me in my first curacy she helped me to see through the situation and was a source of inspiration. She had an amazing mind which was interested in all kinds of things, despite her physical condition; we often talked about clothes and people. I wear my white stole today not simply because it's the Christmas season but because it was the one she liked best.

She knew the town's gossip before I did and she wasn't afraid to speak her mind – she was a genuine free spirit with a faith in God but not afraid to discuss the kinds of doubts that we all have from time to time.

In one of our last conversations I tried to sympathise with her situation by suggesting that it could not be much fun for someone who had led such an active life to be unable to do anything but lie in bed; 'Oh,' she said, 'it's OK because I'm still busy in my mind' – and so she was and that's how I remember her – as a courageous, free spirit who, despite all that life had thrown at her, remained an encourager of others, a pilgrim and busy in her mind until the end.

May she rest in God's eternal peace. Amen.

My father was always a very faithful parish priest who wore his cassock most of the time. He would cycle round the parish with his cassock hitched up in his belt. He tried to visit everyone regularly and when this became more difficult as the numbers increased he got very frustrated. He never drove and when we got a car it was usually my mother who took him. I can also remember helping out during the school holidays.

He was much loved because of his uncomplicated non-judge-mental approach to people. That is not to say that he did not have likes and dislikes. Orsett, his final parish, had a very strong Masonic lodge and there were countless times when people would try to get him to join, but he always refused. But he was respected and the whole village came out to say goodbye at his funeral.

DHG

My first school was Windsor School in Beckton. We lived in the rectory on the corner of Manor Way and Windsor Terrace. The latter led to the main entrance of Beckton Gas Works. The former was the main road from East Ham down to the Royal Docks. It was, and still is, the 101 bus route. The school was near an area called Cyprus, so named presumably for the many Cypriots who lived in the area. We were surrounded by prefabs, the quick, cheap houses that were put up after the war. I seem to remember that they were surprisingly spacious and I would not be surprised if one or two survive today.

My first days at school were not very happy but I do remember my teacher – Mrs Wilkinson – taking me under her wing. I still remember her showing me a picture postcard of St Andrew's Church, Hornchurch, and more specifically the horns that sit high up on the roof of said church. However, I think I must have settled down and become sufficiently confident to get involved in the rough and tumble of life as a five- or six-year-old.

Two incidents illustrate this very well. I seemed to get into scraps with a classmate who I think was called John Beesson. More than once I managed to rip his shirt. My mother was furious and beat me with the slipper. It was just after the war; there was rationing and shirts were expensive.

The second incident involved myself and a friend called Stephen Thompson who was the son of a priest in Hornchurch. We were playing on a very dry piece of waste land which may have been a bomb site, surrounded by houses. We decided to make and light a bonfire. It must have got out of control because the fire brigade were called. Also a policeman who cautioned us and took our names. I was panic-stricken and cried, but Stephen had the presence of mind to tell the policeman that we were not old enough to go to prison!

My parents moved to Great Yeldham in north Essex around 1952/3. We were certainly there for the coronation of Elizabeth II as I can remember being dressed as a clown and sitting on a float. The trouble was that it rained and the colours of my costume, made from crêpe paper, ran. However I did get a prize for being red, white and blue!

We lived in a splendid old rectory which had 30 rooms (I think that included the lavatories, bathroom, attic rooms etc.) and a huge garden. It was a lovely place for my sister and me to grow up in, but it must have been quite a worry for our parents. Gone were the days when the incumbent had both money and servants and the whole place obviously had seen better times. We never used all the rooms and we virtually lived in the spacious yet cosy kitchen with the Rayburn. For many years, until we were put on to the mains, my father had to go into the garden every day and pump the water into a header tank. We lived simply but I never remember going without.

The garden was pretty large and rambling. Again it had seen former glory, but it was a good place to play in. I had tree camps. There was a large pond which had more mud than water, and invariably when friends came to stay they fell in!

I went to the village school which was just opposite the rectory. The head-

Me at about 5 years old with my sister, Barbara who was 2 years younger.

My first school in Beckton, East London. (back row 4th from left)

mistress was called Miss Newton: very much a traditional head-mistress who ran a fairly tight but not unhappy ship. I must have had a cockney accent because Miss Newton got me to pronounce my 'th's accurately. Actually when I went away to school I was teased a bit for my cockney accent, but it has rubbed off.

At the age of ten or eleven I took the 11+ and failed. However, I was allowed to sit an oral exam (presumably because I was a borderline fail) and I can well remember regaling the examiners with my knowledge of the Plantagenets and March (in the Isle of Ely) railway yards! I must have impressed them as I passed and became eligible for Essex to pay the tuition fees for my next school, the King's School in Ely, where I was to spend the next eight years.

My time at boarding school in Ely was from 1956 to 1964, and must have had an influence on my pursuit of the question 'who do I think I am?' Ely itself was, in those days, nothing much to write home about. It is a fenland town but with a most beautiful cathedral which is visible for miles around. The King's School surrounded the cathedral and needless to say my time there was much influenced by cathedral life. I did go for an audition for the cathedral choir but failed to be selected, but I got into the actual school on my written exam. Actually I don't remember being particularly upset about the choir as it would have been quite a commitment of my time and energy.

If it wasn't for the generous Uncle Alec and Essex County Council, my parents would have not been able to afford the school's fees, which invariably went up each year. The school was single-sex and was quite small when I arrived. However the head-master, Ben Fawcett, a good man, did much to increase the reputation of the school. My first housemaster was Mr Saunders ('Sandy'), who was also a good influence on me. I went into one of the junior boarding houses – The Priory – at the age of ten or eleven. I went straight into the third form, which was not easy as most of the other boys had been in the school for two years already and had done two years of French and Latin whereas I had to start from scratch.

I never did very well academically at Ely and seem to remember that I reached my peak when I passed the Common Entrance Exam at the age of 13 and thus went up into the senior school and so School House for the next five years. For some reason I was in the 'A' stream, but I have always felt that I would have done better in the 'B' stream, where I would have been more comfortable. I only achieved five O-levels. But the eight years at the King's School were not wasted and on the whole it was a good experience, even though I do remember getting very depressed at the end of the school holidays at the thought of going back. The life of the cathedral, the plays, even the sport (although cross-country runs in the fens were a bit much, especially with a stitch) and indeed the whole life of the school left me with a grounded education. I was given the wherewithal to stand on my own two feet.

Needless to say Ely Cathedral played an important part in my life. We had morning prayers in the Lady Chapel every day and Eucharist on Sundays. Less formal prayers were held both in Prior

Crauden's Chapel and below it in the Undercroft Chapel. These were opposite School House and next to the priory. I had the privilege of carrying the processional cross at the enthronement of the Bishop of Ely. This experience was marred only by a reprimand from the headmaster for wearing brown shoes rather than black under my cassock!

Another activity in the cathedral that comes to mind is helping to usher at a performance of Benjamin Britten's *War Requiem* as part of the Aldeburgh Festival. And I must also mention our own school performances of various plays, the most notable being Marlowe's *Faustus*, in which I was the Cardinal of Lorraine, and André Obey's *Noah*, in which I wore a papier-mâché head of an elephant! And there was Dorothy L. Sayer's *The Zeal of Thy House*.

The sixth form at The King's School, Ely, in 1964 with our headmaster, Ben Fawcett.

This was a spectacular performance in which a huge basket was lowered from the triforium. My friend, John Maine, played most of the leading parts. When he left he worked in TV and theatre and emigrated to America, where he ended up working for Sony.

It was while I was at Ely that I went with others on a 'grand tour' of Europe in eight days. We dashed from one country to another, but the main objective was to go and see the Passion Play at Oberammergau. That was in 1960.

It must have been during my last year at Ely that I began to consider ordination and when I was 18 I went for selection to the ordained ministry. This was in Sheffield and lasted about three days. Not too surprisingly, I was turned down; at least they said, 'Go and do something else and come back in two years' time.' I was disappointed, but in retrospect it was a sensible decision. The question was, what was the 'something else' I could do?

Well, the next two years I spent working as a student helper with the Mission to Seamen, first in Antwerp and then in Newport, Wales. Needless to say this experience was quite an eye-opener for me. Working in ports must have given me a wider experience of life than staying at a boarding school. My work centred round assisting the padre with ship visiting and helping in the Flying Angel Club. It was a good experience getting involved with the Church's mission to seamen of all nationalities, centred around worship and prayer in the chapel.

After two years I went back to the selection board, this time in St Albans, and was recommended for training to the priesthood. The next hurdle was 'where?' as I had pitifully few academic qualifications.

It was around this time that I took myself to work on a farm in Norway. I went under the auspices of an organisation called 'the British Experiment Association'. The idea was for us to get to know people from and experience other countries. I went on my own to a village called Stordal. The nearest town was Trondheim, about halfway up the Norwegian coast. The farmer and his family were friendly but my Norwegian was virtually nil and their English limited. I remember feeling rather lonely. But I did get some good experience, whether it was cleaning out the cattle sheds, lifting potatoes (mechanically), cutting and threshing wheat or looking after the pigs, one of which I discovered I was eating the following day. I think I got paid (a bit!).

The decision to go to Kelham Theological College near Newark in Nottinghamshire in 1966 made a lot of sense. It offered a preliminary course in order that I might get an A-level which was required for training for ordination. The actual course was four years and was run by the Society of the Sacred Mission, a worldwide Anglican religious community. Fr. Kelly, who founded the order at the end of the 19th century, based it on the Benedictine

I was an Associate at Kelham Theological College.

Mum and myself on the day of my ordination to the preisthood at Southwalk Cathedral.

Rule. Initially it was for missionaries to Korea, but he also saw that there were many men with vocations who did not have the qualifications to enter the ministry. In those days a degree was required and so he set up a theological college at Kelham Hall (an impressive Gilbert Scott house on the banks of the River Trent) and also one in Australia. Having been eight years in boarding school, another five years at this particular theological college would not be much different!

So it was that I spent the next five years living in a religious community of monks. Although we were students and had the usual three terms, we shared the life of the monks. This meant that we spent a lot of time in the beautiful chapel. We did all the chores, whether it was polishing the floors, peeling the potatoes, shovelling coal, gardening etc. When I first went there no one was employed, although latterly a cook was taken on from outside.

We had lectures usually from the monks themselves, but people came from outside. I remember Dr Hunter, from the local hospital for people with learning disabilities, lecturing us on mental illness. He was not a religious man but I remember he began by saying that it is a miracle that most of us are born intact, considering the potential hazards that beset us as we prepare to come into this life. He also said that the amount of psychiatry that is of any use can be put on the back of a postage stamp!

Kelham was a holy place but also well earthed. Borstal boys used to come and play football with the students and I remember visiting residents of a hostel run by the Probation Service in Nottingham. There was discipline but by no means was Kelham humourless. It was unique as far as theological training was concerned and when it closed, a few years after I left, the Anglican Church lost a special place, although it was obviously not everyone's cup of tea.

At the end of the five years I did achieve an A-Level in History and the London Diploma in Theology as well as the General Ordination Examination. It would take 38 years before I got a degree – BA (hons) in Film Studies and History.

It was during two summer holidays that I went to Cyprus and Lebanon. For the former I responded to an advertisement to join a Christian peacemaking team which was due to go to Cyprus. I think it was about 1970. Roy Calvacaressi was a lawyer in Green Street in London who masterminded this team. He had a calling to go to places where there was or had been conflict (he later took a group to Northern Ireland). Cyprus has had, and still does have, its fair share of conflict, mainly because of its strategic position in the Mediterranean.

After an interesting journey from London to Venice by train, I travelled by boat down the Adriatic to Rhodes, through the Corinth Canal, Piraeus and then on to Limassol, where I disembarked. The ship went on to Haifa. It was more comfortable to sleep on deck rather than in the 'aircraft seats'.

I joined the group in a small Turkish Cypriot village called Kidasi about halfway between Limassol and Paphos, up in the hills. It had been first been destroyed in an earthquake and then again in the troubles. The group was international, with a majority of Norwegians, and our task was to try and rebuild the houses but also be a Christian witness. How much peacemaking we achieved is questionable as I seem to remember that we provoked our Greek neighbours into jealousy. Anyway, I enjoyed myself, saw something of Cyprus and made some friends. Two of these friends were Lebanese Christians: Elias and Souheil, who lived in Beirut.

The following year I went to stay with Elias's parents. I flew out with Iraqi Airlines and was able to see something of Beirut before it was destroyed by the vicious civil war a year or so afterwards. Elias and Souheil escaped to the USA and Canada. I am sorry to say that we have lost touch and I never found out what happened to Elias's parents. Beirut was a flourishing capital – the 'Geneva of the Middle East'. I was able to help with ushering at the Baalbeck Music Festival which included Oscar Peterson and Ella Fitzgerald. I visited Damascus, Tyre and Sidon. I also had my first experience of a refugee camp, which was presumably Palestinian.

Before I move on to my curacy in the Old Kent Road, I ought just

Angela and I were also married at St. Dunstan's, Stepney.

to mention some jobs that I took during my school and college holidays. The first was working at the Esso terminal at Purfleet on the Thames. Basically this was to get some money, but my experience here was invaluable in getting to know what work was like beyond my inevitably limited experience so far. I did a range of jobs from being a courier between Purfleet and HQ in Victoria to working out how much oil barges could take, actually helping to pour barrels of crude oil into huge vats in order to make aviation fuel, and helping with assembling pay packets in the finance office. I can always remember thinking how little people got, especially if they had to support a family. Then there was my work as a porter at Orsett Hospital. You name it and I did it! Day and night duty. Finally, I did a placement at St Christopher's Hospice in Sydenham, South London, under Dame Cicely Saunders. It was

Angela with our first born, Hannah.

only for two weeks over one Christmas, helping to care for patients as an auxiliary. People used to say that it must have been a very sad place, but, on the contrary, it was very positive. Needless to say, all these experiences had an invaluable input into my future work as a hospital chaplain.

At Advent 1971 I was made deacon by Bishop John Robinson at the church in which I was to do my first curacy – St Philip with St Mark's, Avondale Square, off the Old Kent Road, South London. The following Michaelmas, I was ordained priest in Southwark Cathedral by Bishops Mervyn Stockwood, David Sheppard and Hugh Montefiore.

Although Avondale Square was south of the River Thames, the people who lived there came from the City of London. The old church had been bombed and a modern one replaced it. St Mark's was a pickle factory.

Although my curacy in this parish was invaluable experience I had a definite interest in hospital chaplaincy. I was able to nurture my desire and interest by covering days off and holidays for the chaplain of King's College Hospital in Denmark Hill. During this time I lived 13 storeys up a tower block which I think was 20 storeys!

It was the custom of the parish to have parish holidays and one of these was a week on the River Thames. We hired two cruisers at Hay's Wharf in Rotherhithe and cruised up as far as Wallingford, where my mother was living, and back. It was all great fun and gave me a taste of river and canal cruising.

After three years I started looking for a full-time hospital chaplaincy job and in 1975 I was appointed as assistant chaplain to Christopher Courtauld at the London Hospital in Whitechapel. This also included Mile End Hospital, where my mother nursed and I was born. My bishop there was the Bishop of Stepney, Trevor Huddleston.

My time at the London was invaluable. The hospital was and is a centre of excellence, primarily serving the people of the East End and Essex. It was good to learn under Chris and to work with an ecumenical team which comprised the local RC priest and a part-time free church chaplain who came from the Whitechapel Mission

The Chaplaincy Team with Bishop Trevor Huddleston at the dedication of the new chaptel at Mile End Hospital.

(Methodist). As well as Sister Pamela, Deaconess Order of St Andrew, who was based at the Royal Foundation of St Andrew with members of the Community of the Resurrection. And then I must not forget the rabbi, Mr Schneider, who came from Gants Hill and visited the Jewish patients but also joined us in meeting the nurses in the school of nursing. Chris Courtauld worked hard and our objective was to visit every inpatient.

We worshipped in three places. The main hospital chapel was off the first-floor corridor and had been reduced in size to extend the clinical laboratories, and so had a large sanctuary and very little room for people! But it served well for Communion services and for the offices and of course for private prayer. On Sunday mornings we commandeered the Clinical Theatre East (a lecture theatre) for a simple ecumenical service. It was always quite a task finding wheelchairs (something which has never changed) and wheeling patients to the service. Then there was the Christian Centre which was in the basement below one of the nurses' homes. This was also used by the Christian Union as well as for midweek Communion services, which were attended by staff.

The Christian Centre was used for all sorts of activities. We had plays and charity lunches, and it was at one of these that Chris introduced me to Angela Woodhouse. She was already an SRN, although I never saw her in uniform as she worked in theatre in Fielden House, which housed the private ward.

I proposed to Angela on Christmas Day 1975 and we were married at St Dunstan's Church, Stepney, on the 29th May 1976. The reception was held on an old paddle steamer, *The Old Caledonian*, which was moored near Charing Cross Bridge, and our honeymoon was at a place called Brela, which was in the old Yugoslavia, now Croatia. We lived in a hospital flat on the ground floor of Gwynne House in Turner Street, next to a pub called the Good Samaritan.

About a year after we were married I had to have an operation with subsequent radiotherapy. I will always remember that I had visited two people with a similar complaint. One of them died and

the other, who happened to be a priest, was very poorly. As I was a member of staff, I had a room in the nurses' sick room, which was at the top of the private wards in Fielden House. Needless to say I was very well treated and was in the hands of experts in their field, and the prayers and support of everyone were indispensable. Even though I was no longer in his diocese, Bishop Mervyn, who must have heard that I was in hospital, wrote to me and afterwards I had a very firm but warm letter from Bishop Trevor saying that Angela and I must take some convalescence, which we did at St David's in Pembrokeshire.

In 1979, we moved to Hastings. Angela was pregnant and I had been appointed chaplain to Hastings Health Authority, which comprised eight hospitals along the coast from Hastings through St Leonards-on-Sea to Bexhill. We bought our first house in St Leonards not long before Hannah was born in one of the hospitals – the Buchanan. William was born at home on the 10th May 1982.

Mum, me and todder Hannah.

Four years later we moved to Gloucester, where I was appointed as chaplain to the Gloucestershire Royal Hospital. After 18 months living in a hospital flat we were able to buy a four-bedroomed Edwardian house not far from the hospital. Needless to say it was good to have a substantial house for two growing Godwins! We needed to have something larger after our attractive but small cottage in St Leonards-on-Sea.

I am always grateful that we were able to get on the housing ladder. We had tried earlier when we were living in the East End. There was a two-up, two-down cottage in Mile End Place, which was reached from the Mile End Road and backed onto the Jewish cemetery. However, we were 'gazumped'! We went down there fairly recently. An oasis and not far from the City. But we were very fortunate to buy our own house, which gave some security for Angela and the children if anything happened to me.

Moving to Gloucester meant that I only had two hospitals in contrast to eight in Sussex. This meant that I did not have to spend so much time travelling from site to site. Gloucester has a good-sized purpose-built chapel with an office and vestry. As with Hastings, I was the first full-time hospital chaplain in the diocese of Gloucester. During the next 20 years I built up a substantial lay visiting team and by the time I retired in 2005 (having worked in the NHS for 30 years), I was responsible for three hospitals but had two full-time and four part-time colleagues. Being one amongst thousands of employees (for every one person who lies in a bed there are three who care for them) meant that I was answerable to the management. This was no bad thing as it kept me on my toes! Not everyone valued chaplaincy, especially if the state was paying for it.

About two years before I retired, I was made an honorary canon of Gloucester Cathedral. This was in recognition of my work for hospital chaplaincy in the diocese. It meant that I had a seat in the cathedral (No. 21). When I retired the bishop wrote to say that I must give up my seat. I felt this was a shame as it was a nice little perk, but it had to be given to a new canon. Now I am officially Canon Emeritus, which sounds grander but really means 'has been'!

Messing About in Boats

*I*am not a very 'boaty' person but I do enjoy water, swimming and being on the sea. My two years with the Mission to Seafarers gave me an insight into things nautical and an interest in boats and docks. When I returned to England from Antwerp, I joined a small cargo vessel, *The City of Hull*, sailing down the River Scheldt past Vlissingen and across to Goole.

My first experience of life on rivers and inland waterways was a parish holiday on the Thames when I was a curate. This gave me a taste, which I wanted to pursue. The relaxing nature of river or canal cruising was a great pleasure, as was exploring the country-side and indeed the towns from a different angle. So at both the London Hospital and the Gloucester Royal, I took members of staff on a narrowboat holiday. And indeed during the first year of our marriage, the year of the drought, 1976, Angela and I hired a narrowboat and cruised the Cheshire Ring. Because of the water shortage this holiday did not go without incident, although we did bring the boat back to base on time. But it did not put me off narrowboating and I became the proud owner of a 50-foot narrow-boat called *The Countryman*.

The circumstances which brought me to this state of ownership are something which I cannot be proud about. In about 1989 Angela and I decided to separate and this gave me the opportunity to buy my own narrowboat and to live on it. I bought it off a musician and his wife but I always assumed that the original owner was a farmer, hence *The Countryman*. It was in the Beeston Cut near Nottingham, so I had to bring it down to Tewkesbury Marina, where it was to be moored. I started down the River Trent and then joined the Trent and Mersey Canal, went through the

Coventry Canal and into Birmingham. Through Gas Street Basin, which had not then been redeveloped, and on to the Stratford Canal. Into Stratford-upon-Avon, past the theatre and then down the River Avon to Tewkesbury.

I expect I was the first hospital chaplain to live on a boat. As I was on call I had to make sure that I had a phone line. I was also able to plug into electricity. The main chores were filling the water tank, replacing the gas cylinders and emptying the 'porta-potty'!

Needless to say *The Countryman* brought me and many others a lot of pleasure, although owning a boat brings a lot of responsibility and expense. The quip that owning a boat is like standing in a cold shower ripping up £20 notes rings quite true. Still, it was a fantasy that I was able to put into experience. When Tewkesbury flooded in 1990, I got calls checking that I was OK, but living on a boat was the best place to be – just like Noah!

Although I enjoyed having Hannah and William with me most weekends, and having friends and relations join me for a meal and to cruise the rivers and the canals, I was lonely, and in 1991 I rejoined Angela and the family on terra firma. We kept the boat for a few more years, moving it up to Saul Junction on the Sharpness Canal, and continued to entertain friends by inviting them for a cruise. Angela provided marvellous catering. We also tried lending *The Countryman* to some people for a nominal sum, but this was not very successful. We finally sold it when it all became too expensive. Again, there is a pertinent quip: the two happiest times in one's life are when one buys a boat and when one sells it!

I have talked a bit about my experience on large boats and small boats, but I must now say something about sailing boats. As I have indicated I am not much of a sailor, but I have had the opportunity to do some sailing, and not least on Christopher Courtauld's yacht, *Duet*. This is a very beautiful boat, made of wood and 100 years old, and so it needs quite a lot of muscle power.

I was invited to join the crew on four occasions. The first voyage was from Glasgow down the River Clyde, through the Crinan

Hannah and William on my boat, The Countryman in Tewkesbury marina, circa. 1991.

Canal and then visiting some of the islands including Mull. We returned via Mallaig to Oban.

The second trip was to Holland. We left Ipswich and sailed down the River Orwell and so into the North Sea and into the North Sea Canal to Amsterdam. Here we had an unscheduled stop of three days, because we had to go into a boatyard and have a brand new bowsprit fashioned. Sailing into the North Sea Canal we had collided with a Dutch trawler. I thought we might be sunk but we got away with a broken bowsprit, which was bad enough. Anyway it was a good opportunity to see something of Amsterdam. We then made our way into the IJsselmeer (formerly known as the Zuiderzee) and visited some of the small towns. We didn't get as far north as hoped due to our 'delay'. On our return we crossed the North Sea by night, which was an interesting experience considering it is the busiest shipping lane in the world.

However, we did arrive safely at 'the haven where we would be' (to quote the psalmist).

The third time, William came with me and met *Duet* at La Trinité on the Brittany coast. We then gradually made our way along the coast, calling in at various harbours, and ended up at Brest. I remember jumping into the open sea and swimming back to the boat, which was drifting away and was unable to wait for me!

My final time on *Duet* was spent staying on it, but up on blocks on dry land! The plan was to sail from Poole to the River Dart, and Angela also came for the first day of the sail. However, as we sailed out of Poole Harbour, the rudder broke so we had no steerage. There was a strong wind and we were going straight for some rocks. It was only thanks to the good seamanship of the rest of the

Relaxing on Duet.

crew (not me; I was in the galley feeling rather sick) that the sails were adjusted so that we were able to tack and turn round. I can't remember what happened then, but I expect we were towed back to Poole. The previous day we had also gone on a short trip and the engine had failed, and certainly we had to be towed back then. Poor Chris; *Duet* was loaned to a sailing trust and they had assured him that *Duet* was in good nick! Anyway we enjoyed ourselves using the boat's inflatable to get around, including a visit to Brownsea Island.

I must finally mention a sailing holiday on a much smaller boat. This was amongst some of the Greek islands with Angela's brother Christopher and William. We sailed with about ten other boats in a flotilla and our boat was a 30-foot yacht called *Ria*. We flew to Lefka and set off to the island of Ithaca, the home of Odysseus. I read *The Odyssey* while on our trip and so was able to identify some of the islands and places that Odysseus visited. There was a heatwave, so it was lovely to be able to just jump off the boat into the sea. A most enjoyable holiday, although I did manage to steer the boat into someone's jetty!

With my latest granddaughter, Emmanuella.

Return to Dresden

*I*n May 2015 I had the opportunity to return to Dresden with my new friend Jane.

But before we talk about Dresden I would like to update you with a bit more personal history. I am the proud grandfather of three granddaughters! Isobel (2001), Elizabeth (2010) and Emmanuella (2014). When I first drafted this memoir, Isobel asked whether she was mentioned, to which I had to admit to the negative. But this is also for them and their offspring, so I am dutifully reprimanded. Isobel is five-eighths German, having a German father and great-grandmother.

Thanks to the wonders of the Internet, I recently discovered another German relative. Her name is Marion Knapp (née Magen) and her grandfather Ludwig was one of my grandfather's brothers. Needless to say we are swapping stories and, not surprisingly, our stories are not dissimilar.

In September 2015 I will have been retired for ten years, and on the 8th August 2015 I celebrated my threescore years and ten by sailing down the Sharpness Canal indulging in a cream tea with 58 friends and relatives. Angela and I have amicably divorced and I now live by myself in a delightful top-floor apartment, with two balconies, in the middle of Gloucester Docks. But I am not alone, having met Jane. We alternate between Gloucester and her home in East London, not far from my childhood homes.

Last year (2014) I made two important journeys. The first was to Geneva in Switzerland, where I was able to sprinkle the ashes of my late sister, Barbara-Anne, on Lake Geneva. Barbara-Anne was a strong, fiercely independent person and in many ways took on the pain and suffering of our mother. There has been some documentation about second-generation Holocaust survivors and I feel that Barbara-Anne was one such person. Our mother once told us that she had swum across Lake Geneva and so I thought it appropriate to take Barbara-Anne's remains there. My cousin Jean, who lives in Geneva, found a suitable private spot where a river runs into the lake, so her ashes were carried out into the middle.

Soon after our mother's death, my sister visited Inge, our mother's cousin, in Franklin, Tennessee. I was able to make this same journey in 2014. It was good to meet Inge finally. She is a sprightly 91-year-old who still lives by the kindergarten that she set up in 1952. We were able to exchange stories about our respective families. Inge has written an autobiography and made a DVD about her remarkable life beginning in Dresden.

Another person, no relation this time, but with a similar story which originates in pre-war Dresden, is Monica Petzal. I have yet to meet Monica, who is an artist and lives in Suffolk, but we are in touch and again exchange stories. Her most recent work is *The Dresden Project*, which not only explores her own family narrative within a specific historical context but also contains an exhibition for Dresden's twin city, Coventry.

Jane and I visited Dresden and I was amazed to see how much Dresden has been transformed. Both the bombing in 1945 and the subsequent prosaic rebuilding by the German Democratic Republic left the city a pale reflection of what was a beautiful city, 'the Florence of the Elbe'. However, rebuilding and restoration, especially since the collapse of the GDR in 1989, have restored Dresden to something of its former glory. This is well illustrated by the complete rebuilding of the Frauenkirche – the Church of Our Lady – in the centre of Dresden. When we visited before in 1997, there was a heap of rubble, but the people of Dresden did possess all the original plans and after much controversy it was decided to rebuild. The motto for this remarkable restoration project is 'Building bridges, living reconciliation, strengthening faith'. The people of Coventry have given the new gold cross which proudly stands on the dome of the Frauenkirche. Also a copy of the Cross of Nails – which came from the old destroyed Coventry Cathedral – is displayed inside the church.

As far as my personal family history is concerned, I have made a start but will have to go back to Dresden at a later date. I discovered the whereabouts of the Jewish cemetery where my grandfather's remains may lie and where Eduard and Martha Hinzelmann are buried, but was unable to get there. However, we did drive down the road where the Magen family lived. This used to be called Fürstenstrasse (Princes Street) but was renamed Fetscherstrasse by the GDR. One could not have references to royalty in a communist state! The original houses, including No. 18, are no longer there; whether bombed or pulled down I am not certain. In their place are prosaic structures, presumably built during the communist era.

The aforenamed Monica has told me about a project called *Stolpersteine* ('Stepping Stones' or 'Stumbling Blocks'). This, according to its website (http://www.stolpersteine.eu/en/), is:

> An art project that commemorates the victims of National Socialism, keeping alive the memory of all Jews, Roma and Sinti, homosexuals, dissidents, Jehovah's Witnesses and victims of euthanasia who were deported and exterminated.

The idea is that on the pavement outside 18 Fürstenstrasse, I could get an artist called Gunter Demnig to engrave, on a brick each, the names of my family. I feel this would be a very fitting memorial to the Magens. My personal project is very much a work in progress but will definitely mean a return visit to Dresden and indeed to Chemnitz to see whether their house and pharmaceutical works still exist.

So, Who Do I Think I Am?

*T*he debate about whether it is nature or nurture that most influences who we are is never going to go away. There is always going to be the temptation to emphasise one rather than the other. The fact is that we are a mixture and that most of us are, in my mother's words, 'mongrels'.

I think that it is clear that my genes are a mixture of Godwin (whether I am a descendant of King Harold, son of Earl Godwin, we shall never know, but it is fanciful speculation!) and Magen. As I never knew any of my grandparents and neither my father nor my mother spoke of them in any great detail, I can only speculate. Looking at general characteristics, I should say that I am more Godwin than Magen. I look more like my father than my mother and I think I behave more like my father than my mother. I can't say that I have inherited the intellect of my grandfather, Kurt Magen, but perhaps I am a bit of a loner, as I think he was, and also share his dislike of being told what to do!

More seriously and indeed importantly, I would like to consider my Jewish heritage.

Quite frankly, it was only when I first received that letter from the International Red Cross in 1997 and subsequently visited Dresden that I came aware of my Jewish roots. I suppose that I did know about them before but they were very much on the 'back burner' of my consciousness. I certainly did not show any interest or concern. It was something that did not particularly bother me. I knew a bit about Jewish history through reading and studying the Old Testament. I had studied the Second World War a bit and was, of course, aware of the Holocaust. As I have already said, my mother did not discuss these things and her Jewish heritage was by no means a priority. On the contrary she denied it, and who is to blame her? So I had no personal interest or curiosity.

Yet seeing the photograph of my mother as a teenager with her sister and parents brought home to me that I am inexorably connected to my mother's family. It was a sort of confirmation of a fact that up until then meant very little to me. That I have Jewish blood cannot and should not be denied, although I understand that the Magen family, along with thousands of other German Jews, denied their Jewishness in order to try and survive. It is possible that the family were baptised (my mother possessed a Lutheran hymn book) in the hope of escaping.

Then there was Kurt himself. There is no indication that he was an attender of the synagogue, and Klemperer's description of him as

Jane and me at the top of the Shard.

the 'Jewish pharmacist' is not a description, I imagine, he would have endorsed. But I may be wrong. His ashes were interred in the Jewish cemetery in Dresden.

Renee Woodhouse, the Jewish second wife of Angela's father, urged me to be proud of my Jewish roots. Yes, I am, but that is not the be-all and end-all. Although I admire and am proud of all the Jewish people have achieved down the ages in the face of unimaginable prejudice, and of my own family's achievement, there is also a sense that I must move on.

Let me try and explain. Bishop Hugh Montefiore described

William, his wife Emma and Emmanuella.

himself as a 'Jewish Christian', and that seems a very apt description of me. However, he was brought up as Jewish and converted to Christianity. I was brought up as a Christian, and believe that Jesus is the Messiah. I also believe that to understand Christianity and the New Testament it is also necessary to understand the Jewish people and their history as revealed in the Old Testament. The Old Testament has been described as 'salvation history', a history which is about God's relationship with the Jewish people.

I sometimes feel that there is no future for the Jewish faith as it stands. Of course there is a great tradition, which I love and respect, and they are indeed the Chosen People. But that also brings a huge responsibility to be true to their faith in God. To me the term 'secular Jew' is almost a misnomer. And to rely on tradition is not enough. The song 'Tradition' in the show *Fiddler on the Roof* brings out this mournful fact. The organisation 'Jews for Jesus' does seem to be more positive. They claim that Jesus is the Messiah but also respect Jewish culture and tradition, which is, I hope, what all of us should be doing.

There is an old joke that wherever you have five Jews arguing, there will be six opinions! That is how it seems to me. I heard on the radio two rabbis arguing, one Orthodox and the other Reformed, about whether the Jewish line should be recognised through the father as well as, traditionally, the mother.

Hannah, her husband Craig, Isobel and Elizabeth.

It was necessary that I should visit Israel and I have had the privilege to visit three times. Always as part of a pilgrimage organised by McCabe Travel, who specialise in pilgrimages to the Holy Land. The first time was just after the First Gulf War, which was good because there were not many other tourists around crowding up the holy places. The second time I co-led the pilgrimage, which was quite a responsibility, and the third time Angela came with me. So we were able to tread in the footsteps of Jesus, but also visit many Old Testament and New Testament sites and Jewish sites such as Masada, impressive Roman remains such as Caesarea and Crusader sites such as Acre.

Of course, we also visited modern Israel and Palestine. I visited a kibbutz and Yad Vashem (the Holocaust museum), and on our most recent visit we also saw something of the Palestinian plight on the West Bank and, sadly, the newly constructed security wall. I think we visited St George's Anglican Cathedral in Jerusalem every time, which it must be remembered is staffed by Israeli Arabs. The Christian in Israel is indeed 'between a rock and a hard place'!

Altogether McCabe were careful to give us a balanced view of what is happening in the Holy Land. Each time we stayed both in an Arab hotel by the walls of old Jerusalem and in an Israeli hotel on the banks of the Sea of Galilee.

My friend Jane worked in the Hadassah Hospital in Jerusalem when she was younger, and we hope to visit Israel again and see the famous Chagall windows in the synagogue there. I find Chagall fascinating as he does not shy away from bringing together both Jewish and Christian symbolism. His painting *The White Crucifixion* is a prime example. Anything that brings Christians and Jews together is essential, not least as we see the rise of anti-Semitism once again. The root and, indeed, the perpetuating of such evil stands squarely in the Christian camp. Great proponents of Christianity, such as John Chrysostom, Bishop of Constantinople in the 5th century, or Martin Luther in the 16th century, have much to answer for in their anti-Semitic statements.

There needs to be continued dialogue between the two faiths because we are so close yet still so far apart. Organisations such as the Council of Christians and Jews do much to facilitate understanding and cooperation.

To look into one's and other people's pasts is, to my mind at least, always fascinating. As with the study of history, I hope that we will always be able to learn something about ourselves and to understand perhaps a bit more clearly why such and such a thing happened or why we behave in such a way. One indisputable fact is that if it wasn't for Hitler I would not be here. God does indeed work in mysterious ways.

Bibliography

Haase, Norbert, Stefi Jersch-Wenzel and Hermann Simon (eds). *Die Erinnerung hat ein Gesicht: Fotografien und Dokumente zur national-sozialistischen Judenverfolgung in Dresden 1933–1945.* Prepared by Marcus Gryglewski. Leipzig, 1998

Hirsch, Ernst, and Ulrich Teschner. *Die Juden sind weg. Das Lager Dresden Hellerberg* (video)

Weg der Erinnerung: Dresden 23rd November 1997 (video)

Johnson, Paul. *A History of the Jews.* London: Weidenfeld & Nicolson, 2004

Klemperer, Victor. *I Shall Bear Witness: The Diaries of Victor Klemperer 1933–41.* Trans. Martin Chalmers. London: Weidenfeld & Nicolson, 1998

Klemperer, Victor. *To The Bitter End: The Diaries of Victor Klemperer 1942–45.* Trans. Martin Chalmers. London: Weidenfeld & Nicolson, 1999

Klemperer, Victor. *The Lesser Evil: The Diaries of Victor Klemperer 1945–59.* Trans. Martin Chalmers. London: Weidenfeld & Nicolson, 2003

Montefiore, Hugh. *On Being a Jewish Christian.* London: Hodder & Stoughton, 1998

Silverman, Ingrid. *Auf den Spuren der Menschen der 'Judensiedlung' am Hellerberg in Dresden 23.11.1942–03.03.1943.* 1997

Smith, Inge, and Pam Horne. *Born for America: The Life of Inge Meyring Smith.* Franklin, Tennessee: O'More, 2012

Appendix I: Father and Son

A screenplay for a docu-drama about Kurt and Claus Magen.

TITLE OVER: 'FATHER AND SON'

Archive black-and-white footage of historic Dresden before it was bombed.

FADE FROM BLACK

SUPERIMPOSE: 'During World War II, Victor Klemperer, a German Jewish professor, managed to live and survive in Dresden. He secretly wrote his diaries, which describe the persecution of the Jews in that city.'

INT. BEDSIT FLAT – NIGHT

VICTOR KLEMPERER, middle-aged, short-sighted man sitting at a table writing a diary in a sparsely furnished one-room flat. There is a curtain, which separates the sleeping area.

> VICTOR KLEMPERER (VO)
> 26th May, Tuesday morning.
> I often heard of a Jewish pharmacist called Magen. The man was arrested several times. His 17-year-old son fled as he was about to be evacuated and evidently escaped. That was in January. As a result the father – a 50-year-old

– was arrested again; he was put in the familiar solitary confinement of the police cells …

SUPERIMPOSE: 'Dr Kurt Magen and Claus, father and son, were caught up in Hitler's Final Solution. This film is based on their story.'

DISSOLVE TO:

EXT. MAGEN'S HOUSE – DAY

KURT, a tall portly man with glasses, and his wife ERNA, who is also tall and well dressed, greet their teenage children as they get out of a taxi, loaded with three school trunks; ANNELIES, STEFFI and CLAUS are also quite tall and slim. The girls greet their parents enthusiastically; Claus is more reticent. The driver unloads their school trunks. Kurt, rather formally, greets the children by shaking hands. Erna hugs each one in turn.

                    KURT
    How was your journey? You're late. Did you have trouble
    at the border?

                    ANNELISE
    Not at all, Father. We just asked the driver to stop for
    lunch at that picnic site by the lake and then forgot the
    time. Claus and I could not resist going for a swim. I hope
    you are not too cross.

INT. DRAWING ROOM – DAY

A well-furnished drawing room with a large fireplace and French windows through which one can see a lawn with a tennis court.

The family settle down by the fire, while tea is served by a uniformed maid. Erna is sitting on a sofa between her daughters. Dr Magen sits in a comfortable armchair close to the fireplace in which a log fire is burning, while Claus stands with his back to them all looking out of the French windows. They start to talk.

                          KURT
    I'm afraid you will not be able to go back to St Gallen next
    term. Life is getting difficult here. I have been told that I
    cannot send any more money out of the country for your
    school fees.

                      KLEMPERER (VO)
    The Magen family were comfortably off. Magen was a
    very successful pharmacologist and owned his own
    works in Chemnitz. He had gained his PhD at Zurich
    University and had served an apprenticeship with IG
    Faben – an irony because they later produced the gas
    used for exterminations. Dr Magen had subsequently
    built up his own successful business.

PHOTOGRAPHS OVER: Still photographs of Kurt Magen, his wife and two daughters, posing for the camera, on a Sunday afternoon trip to the mountains in Czechoslovakia.

A separate snapshot of Claus.

EXT. TEGEL AIRPORT, BERLIN – DAY

The Magen family saying goodbye to Annelies, as she boards a plane. They are standing at the foot of the steps going up to the twin-propeller plane. Annelies, with a suitcase at her feet, hugs her mother and sister and shakes hands with her father. Claus's attention is elsewhere; he is looking at the plane. His father calls and beckons for him to come and say goodbye to his sister.

ANNELIES (crying)
You *will* come and see me in England soon. It would be lovely if you could send me my bike.

KURT (slowly)
As soon as we can, we will come and join you. My plan is to meet you in Liverpool and then we'll all take a boat to Australia.

Archive footage of train leaving Neustadt station, Dresden.

KLEMPERER (VO)
The Gestapo soon put Hitler's orders into practice, starting with deportation and then moving on to concentration camps and extermination. Although it was possible for Magen's daughter Annelies to go to England thanks to the Quakers, the plan for the rest of the family to join her never materialised.

Archive footage on black-and-white 8mm film of the last 300 Jews assembling in Dresden. They are being processed through a decontamination centre and then being billeted in a camp for Jews. The film ends with trains arriving at Auschwitz.

KLEMPERER (VO)
Dr Magen's wife, Erna, and her remaining daughter, Steffi, were soon to be rounded up along with the remaining Jews of Dresden and forced to go to the Jews' camp in the Hellerberg district. The younger people were made to work in the Zeiss Ikon works making intricate parts for armaments. But after six months, they were all transported to Auschwitz. And then Dr Magen himself

was arrested and put into solitary confinement in the central police headquarters in Dresden. Claus, his son, was deported to Riga, Latvia.

INT. PRISON CELL – DAY
A prison cell with a tiny window which lets in very little light. There is a mattress on the floor. Dr Magen lies on this trying to read a book.

The door opens and two Gestapo men lead Dr Magen out of the cell.

> GUARD (as they lead him away)
> The commandant would like to have a few words with you.

INT. PRISON INTERVIEW ROOM – DAY

A plain room, with no windows, set up for interrogation. There is a large sink in the corner with a dripping tap. The COMMANDANT sits at a table with Dr Magen sitting opposite him. The two guards stand behind him. A light shines into Dr Magen's face.

> COMMANDANT (not aggressively)
> Do you know why we have brought you here?

> KURT
No!

> COMMANDANT (more facetious)
> Well, I am surprised. I thought you were supposed to be clever. You certainly seem to have done pretty well. Just like all the other bloody Jews in this town!

KURT (very matter-of-fact; unemotional)
I'm German just like you. I fought in the last war; did
you? I was awarded the Iron Cross. Were you?

Guard punches Kurt in the face. His glasses go flying. He falls to
the floor and slowly pulls himself up onto the chair.

COMMANDANT
You asked for that.

(continues, looking at some papers)

You don't seem to have cooperated with your betters.
Surely you know that joining the Freemasons is banned?

Kurt stares ahead, silent.

COMMANDANT (trying to be more friendly)
Let's get to the point. You are a clever man, Dr Magen,
and we know that you have invented all sorts of pills and
potions. We also know that you are developing a formula
which could be very useful for us …

KURT (interrupting)
I am not interested in giving you any of my information.
You can have my head but not what is in it.
COMMANDANT
In that case we will have to try another approach.

(to the guards)

Take him away and start by not giving him anything to
eat or drink. Oh, yes, and a bit of sleep deprivation will
help.

INT. PRISON CELL – DAY

Dr Magen is lying on his mattress when the guards burst in. They order him to get up and go with them, but he is too weak to raise himself. So they roughly pull him up and drag him out of the cell between them.

> KLEMPERER (VO)
> For the next few weeks, Dr Magen was systematically interrogated and beaten. But he refused to give any information.

INT. INTERROGATION ROOM – DAY

Magen being interrogated with the light full in his face. When there is no response, the guards punch him in the face and beat his body with lumps of wood. He collapses on the floor. He is hauled up onto the chair, questioned again and the beatings continue.

INT. PRISON CELL – NIGHT

The guards enter the cell dragging Dr Magen between them and they throw him onto the mattress. He lies there lifeless.

FADE TO:

INT. TRAIN CORRIDOR – DAY
Claus Magen in a crowded carriage full of children, standing in the corridor with his head hanging out of the window. A train guard approaches and pulls him inside, remonstrating with him. As soon as the guard leaves, Claus continues to lean out of the window.

KLEMPERER (VO)

In the meantime, Magen's son was crammed in a train with hundreds of other children, destined for Riga. It was his intention that he would jump from the train at the earliest opportunity. This occurred as the train stopped at the German border.

EXT. OUTSIDE STATIONARY TRAIN – NIGHT

A carriage door opens and Claus jumps out of the train onto the tracks. He spots a soldier with a dog in the distance and immediately crouches underneath the train and disappears.

EXT. OPEN COUNTRYSIDE – DAY

Claus is running through pastoral land, occasionally looking behind him. He stumbles and falls, but immediately picks himself up and continues, panting.

EXT. FOREST – DAY

Claus walking with difficulty through a dense forest. He is beginning to look dishevelled and distressed. He comes to a small track and looks both ways, trying to work out which way he should go. He realises that he is lost and collapses on his haunches.

EXT. HAYSTACK – NIGHT

Claus is asleep in a haystack. Suddenly there is the barking of dogs. He wakes and sits up listening and peering intently into the night. The barking stops and he goes back to sleep.

EXT. MOUNTAIN STREAM – DAY

Claus is drinking from a stream. He is kneeling with one hand scooping up the water to drink. He is looking exhausted. He gets up and looks at the distant Alps and continues towards them with a new spring in his step.

EXT. EDGE OF THE RIVER RHINE – DAY

Claus stands by the river edge looking this way and that, not quite certain what to do. Three barges approach, and when the third has just passed he dives in behind it and starts swimming frantically. Suddenly a figure with a gun appears out of the third barge's wheelhouse. He is a soldier and starts shooting at Claus with an automatic weapon. For a moment it looks as if Claus may escape the bullets hitting the water all around him, as the barge is still moving and the soldier is losing range. A second soldier appears with a rifle and after three shots, Claus is wounded; the back of his shirt is covered with blood, but he still tries to swim. The barge has stopped and has managed to manoeuvre close enough for the soldier and a colleague to haul Claus aboard. Claus tries to resist arrest but is easily overpowered by the soldiers.

INT. IN THE BACK OF A COVERED ARMY TRUCK – NIGHT

Claus, bleeding, has been forced to lie on his front between two soldiers in the back of a lorry. One of the soldiers sits with his feet on Claus's back.

EXT. OUTSIDE THE POLICE HQ IN DRESDEN – DAY

Army lorry drives up and Claus is bundled out of the lorry and into Police HQ. His wound is still bleeding and he has to be helped by the guards.

INT. COMMANDANT'S OFFICE – DAY

The commandant is sitting in his chair. Dr Kurt Magen is dragged in by two guards. He is thoroughly battered and bruised. He is pushed into the chair in front of the commandant. The commandant then slowly and dramatically bends down and opens a drawer of his desk. He is looking smugly at his victim and produces Claus's bloodstained shirt, which he throws on the desk with a flourish.

> COMMANDANT
> Right, we have some news for you. Your son tried to escape from the transport train. He was caught trying to get to Switzerland. But he is back with us now. I thought you might like to see this.

The commandant gestures at the shirt on the desk.

> COMMANDANT (continued)
> Do you recognise this?

Kurt slowly nods several times. It is Claus's shirt.

> COMMANDANT (continued)
> We will let him go if you give me the formula.

Kurt talks wearily to the commandant, who listens intently, taking notes.

KURT

What do you want to know; where do I start? . . .

His speech becomes more distant and although we can hear him talking we cannot hear what he is saying. The guards then take him back to his cell.

Archive black-and-white footage of people loaded in cattle trucks being transported to Auschwitz, where they disembark.

KLEMPERER (VO)

In fact they double-crossed Dr Magen. Claus was taken to Auschwitz anyway, where he perished, as did his mother, Erna, and his sister, Steffi.

Still black-and-white photographs (mugshots) of Claus at Auschwitz. Also close-up of his name and details from the Auschwitz records.

Pictures of his mother and sister (in the Hellerberg camp).

INT. PRISON CELL – DAY

Dr Magen lying on the mattress, very weak. A guard comes in and speaks.

GUARD (bluntly)

Your son has been taken to Auschwitz.

FADE OUT

INT. VICTOR KLEMPERER'S FLAT – DAY

Klemperer, writing his diary, as before. Close-up of the page.

KLEMPERER (VO)
… 'Magen has died.' – 'One murder more! (with irony)
'But no! They don't do things like that at the Police Praesidium, they behave properly there. He simply had heart
trouble and won't have got any treatment there.' So this
is no longer considered a murder but a normal end …

KLEMPERER (thinking – VO)
I wonder if he took his own life; he had the wherewithal
to do it.

BLACK OUT

Appendix II: Notices

Amtliche Bekanntmachungen

Personalien

Barmizwoh:

In der Synagoge, Zeughausstraße 1b

1. Mai 1937: Peter Bauer, Sohn des Bankbeamten Herrn Henry Bauer, Zinzendorfstraße 9.

Trauung:

4. April 1937: Frl. Edith Feingold, Dresden, Stephanienstr. 35, mit Herrn Dipl.-Kfm. Hugo Goldmann, Hindenburg.

Sterbefälle:

26. März 1937: Frau Franziska Lichtenstern, Werderstr. 35.
27. März 1937: Herr Paul Levi, Bayreuther Straße 42.
31. März 1937: Herr Alexander Buckwitz, Grunaer Straße 22.
10. April 1937: Frau Martha Hinzelmann, Fürstenstr. 18

Personalnotiz:

Am 4. 4. 1937 verschied in Tel Aviv Herr Siegfried Plonkowski, ein früheres verdientes Vorstandsmitglied unserer Gemeinde.

Obituary notice for Martha Hinzelmann.

K.=L. Buchenwald

Magen   Kurt   Häftlings-Nr. 23282

(Vor- und Zuname)

geb. am 9. 7. 82   zu Leobschütz   Fahrgeld

Datum	Zugang		Abgang		Bestand		
	RM	Rpf	RM	Rpf	RM	Rpf	
30. 11. 38	20	—			20	—	vom M. drehen
1. 12.			20	—	—	—	Karl Magen
28. 11. 38	20.	—			20.	—	vom M. drehen (mit doppelte St.)
	40.	—	20.	—	20.	—	Ma gut
15 Okt. 1940			20.	—	—.	—	s. Akt.
	40,	—	40.	—	—.	—	

Übertrag:

No. 9 R. Borkmann, Weimar

Record of Karl Magen in Buchenwald.

Laufende Nr.	Zu- und Vornamen des Verstorbenen	Geburtstag und Ort	Todestag und Sterbeort	Letzter Wo
82651	*Pietsch,* *Frig. Maria Louisa* *geb. Ender*	7. 9. 76 *Leutomitz*	24. 5. 42 *Gr.*	*Leutpr.*
82652	*Schütz,* *Karl Friedrich*	17. 7. 12 *Naumer*	25. 5. 42 *Radeberg*	*Gespers*
82653	*Hönel,* *Helene Irene* *geb. Seidel*	29. 9. 91 *Goldberg*	24. 5. 42 *Gr.*	*Cormes*
82654	*Braun,* *Irta Emma*	25. 10. 76 *Erlbach*	24. 5. 42 *Gr.*	*Erlbach*
82655	*Maier,* *Maximilian Johann*	25. 5. 54 *König*	27. 5. 42 *Gr.*	*Zeller*
82656	*Pichler,* *Josef*	24. 1. 57 *Rablitz*	25. 5. 42 *Gr.*	*Wien Nr. 3*
82657	Magen, *Karl Israel*	9. 7. 12 Leutschütz	23. 5. 42 *Gr.*	*Schützenpl. Nr. 2*
82658	*Neubert,* *Auguste Martha* *geb. König*	29. 4. 64 *Preußisch-Holland*	27. 5. 42 *Gr.*	*Freiburg*
82659	*Kleindienst,* *Heinrich Karl + Emil* *Konrad Hermann Ernst*	8. 7. 68 *Freilsheim*	27. 5. 42 *Neuerode*	*Zeller*
82660	*Schreiter,* *Robert Max*	24. 10. 66 *Geisau*	26. 5. 42 *Instal*	*Jusila*

Karl Magen "cremation record".

			Name			geb.	
	Erh	44249	Podsadlo	Johann		geb. 19.2.05	
2		44269	Fisior	Eduard		11.3.01	
8		44712	Adamiec	Georg		7.7.25	
9		45047	Kobos	Vinzenz		9.8.17	
	Franz	45656	Fourmentin	Karl		9.2.98	
1		45913	Moutard	Andree		25.4.03	
2		45970	Perrottot	Rene		20.5.21	
3		45972	Pesson	Daniel		25.2.03	
4		46150	Stephan	Franz		19.5.08	
5		46161	Fröllert	Leo		21.5.01	
6	Poll.Jude	47330	Hirschneder	Erich Isr.		10.6.02	
7		47344	Katz	Leo Isr.		19.2.11	
8	Russe	48876	Solomatin	Anatolij		25.2.13	
9		49771	Czcizornyj	Peter		- . - . 23	
30	Pole	51435	Ciszuski	Siegmund		23.4.19	
1		57043	Bieniaszczyk	Franz		28.9.99	
2		6963	Friedrich	Max		18.11.20	
3	St. Jude	33362	Bochner	Isidor Isr.		25.4.24	
4	Pole	34048	Gregorczyk	Peter		18.7.89	
5	St. Jude	36458	Winkler	Zoltan Isr.		4.7.07	O
6		36650	Blau	Maximilian Isr.		14.12.10	
7		57032	Kochen	David Isr.		2.5.21	
8	Pole	57781	Jazierski	Stanislaus		10.4.99	
9	Jude	39895	Magen	Klaus Isr.		8.12.23	
40	Frz. --	40952	Labovici	Leo Isr.		24.11.02	
1		41816	Berger	Abraham Isr.		11.11.04	
2		41962	Ehsterman	Szmul Isr.		11.11.09	
3		42625	Proger	Pinkus Isr.		5.10.03	
4		42852	Borowka	Julius Isr.		24.4.08	
5		43231	Künstler	Maier Isr.		17.6.08	
6		43253	Landau	Oser Isr.		20.12.08	

Record of Claus Magen's Auschwitz record.

Nr. 21731/1942   729

Auschwitz, den ___ 25. August _____ 19

D er Schlosserlehrling Claus Joachim Eduard Israel M

_____ evangelisch, früher mosaisch _____

wohnhaft Dresden, Altenzellerstraße Nr. 26 _____

ist am 16. August 1942 _____ um __14__ Uhr __10__ Minu

in Auschwitz, Kasernenstraße _____ verstorb

D er Verstorbene war geboren am 8. Dezember 1923 _____

in Chemnitz _____

(Standesamt _____ Nr. _____

Vater: Kurt Israel Magen _____

Mutter: Erna Sara Magen geborene Hinzelmann, wohnhaft _

in Dresden _____

D ~~Verstorbene war nicht verheiratet~~

Eingetragen auf ~~mündliche~~ — schriftliche Anzeige des Arztes Doktor der

Medizin Meyer in Auschwitz vom 16. August 1942 _____

D ~~Anzeigende~~

~~Vorgelesen, genehmigt und unterschi~~

Die Übereinstimmung mit dem
Erstbuch wird beglaubigt.

Auschwitz, den 25. 8. 19 42

Der Standesbeamte   **Der Standesbeamte**
In Vertretung   In Vertretung
                                         Quakernack

Todesursache Akuter Magendarmkatarrh

Eheschliessung de ___ Verstorbenen am _____ in _____

(Standesamt _____ Nr. _____

Claus Magen's death certificate.